W9-CUF-263

LOGGING ROAD TRAVEL

Curved bridge along Port Renfrew - Shawnigan logging road provides unexpected thrill for first-time travellers.

LOGGING ROAD TRAVEL
with
Alec and Taffy Merriman

VOLUME ONE
VICTORIA TO CAMPBELL RIVER

with maps and sketches
by Nelson Dewey

Copyright © 1973, 1975 All Rights Reserved
by Alec Merriman
and Saltaire Publishing Ltd.
P.O. Box 2003, Sidney, B.C.

Revised with Additions — 1975

All rights reserved, including the rights to reproduce this book, or parts thereof, in any form. No material in this book may be used without the written permission of the publisher or the copyright owner.

PRINTED IN CANADA

Other books by the author:

- Outdoors with Alec Merriman, revised with Outdoor Calendar and Freshwater Fishing Guide.

- How to Catch Steelhead!

- Logging Road Travel
    Volume I
    Victoria to Campbell River

- Logging Road Travel
    Volume II
    Campbell River to Cape Scott

- Salmon Fishing With the Experts

CONTENTS

Threshold of New Era 9

Gulf Island Adventure 16
By Land and Sea

Outdoor Meals 26
In Winter Months

Highlands Roads 34
Close To Home

MacMillan Bloedel Opens Roads 38
For Full Time Recreational Use

Sooke-Port Renfrew 42
Victoria's Playground

Colwood-Jordan River Side Trips 46
For Beaches and Salmon Fishing

Gateway To West Coast 50

Jordan River To Port Renfrew 52
For Hiking Trails and Beaches

Harris Creek Steelhead Pools 60
Along Cowichan Lake Shortcut

Bear Creek - Shawnigan 64
Rugged But Enticing

Sooke Logging Roads Give 70
Access To 230 Square Miles

Through Historic Leechtown 75

Butlers To Weeks Lake 76

Sooke Lakes Hold Promise 80

Loop Roads In All Directions 84
In MB's Shawnigan Division

Deerholme Mainline   84

Loop to Weeks Lake and   88
Renfrew Road

Loop From Skutz Falls   90

Loop to Wild Dear, Koksilah   92

Cowichan Lake Circle Trip   94

Skyline Road To Nitinat   102

River Campground and Tuck Lake   106

Enter Nitinat From Cowichan Lake   110

Follow River To Campground   112

Canoe Nitinat Triangle Lakes   114

MacMillan Bloedel Provides   116
Wilderness Camping Spots

West Coast Trail   122
Starts at Pachena
... ocean fishing at Bamfield

Barkley Sound   126
for Fishing, Cruising

Sarita River, Lake   130
For Camping-Fishing

Nitinat River to Alberni   134
... and Big Tyee Salmon

Lake-Studded Circle Trip   136
From Great Central Lake

MORE . . .

CONTENTS

Nahmint Watershed
Blueprint for Future   144

Drive Up Mount Arrowsmith
Ski, Fish and Hunt   150

Nanaimo Lakes Road
To Steelhead Pools   154

System of Trout-Filled Lakes
Behind Crown Zellerbach Gate   158

Two Access Routes Lead
To Lakes Back of Nanaimo   162

Blackjack Always Open
But Can Be Rough   163

Northwest Bay Access
Easiest To Boomerang   168

Spider Lake For Bass
Horne Lake For Trout   170

Courtenay Playground
Shown In New CZ Map   174

Circle Trip
Cowichan to Nanaimo   176

See Oyster River
From Logging Roads   178

Maps   182

THRESHOLD OF A NEW ERA

As this book goes to press recreational use of logging roads in British Columbia is on the threshold of a new era.

Logging road travel for outdoor recreationists on Vancouver Island has only been a pursuit to be enjoyed by the average outdoorsmen in the past decade.

During that time thousands of miles of logging road have been opened for recreation use during non-operating hours on a program of shared use with the timber companies. Since the first edition of this book some companies, mainly MacMillan Bloedel, have opened their inactive and mainline logging roads for recreation travel on an all hours seven-days a week basis.

When we started writing an outdoors column in 1960 all logging roads on Vancouver Island were gated against general public use.

The only recreational access to the forestlands was through a limited number of gates where fish and game clubs had made arrangements for hunting access for their members. Those gates were manned during weekend hours by fish and game club members, and then only from 6 a.m. until 3 p.m. during the hunting season.

There was no general public access except for Crown Zellerbach operations in the Nanaimo Lakes area where company officials manned the gates and allowed the public to enter during regulated times under a permit system.

But, fish and game clubs had maintained all along they sought full public access for all purposes — hunting, fishing, hiking, boating, exploring.

They jeopardized their own membership rolls and

revenues by continuing to fight for public access and a sharing in the use of the forestlands.

In 1962 they started to win their fight and legislative public access hearings were held during the sitting of the legislature ... and it was a knock-em-down-drag-em-out affair. Feelings ran high.

The top brass of the major logging companies attended the hearings and presented their stands. The Nanaimo Fish and Game Club and the Victoria Fish and Game Club carried the ball for all recreationists ... and to them we owe our thanks for the recreational opportunities we enjoy in the forests today.

The companies presented some stiff opposition, but the hearings broke wide open when the Victoria Fish and Game Club representatives, upon being challenged by then Forests Minister Ray Williston to show where they were being kept from forestlands, presented a letter from a company official, explaining that the company could not provide hunter access to the fish and game clubs because there were just enough deer in the area to satisfy company employee hunters.

From then on things got better for the recreationists.

The result was an Industrial Roads Act which gave logging companies some protection when the public used the logging roads.

The fish and game clubs had sought a public access act from the legislature, but the companies said they would rather work out the public access problems themselves ... and pledged to do so.

It was left at that ... and from then on the public access and multiple use program started to develop.

The results are shown by the thousands of miles now used by recreationists.

Multiple use started to work on Vancouver Island, and in the rest of British Columbia ... not the full shared program recreationists seek, but a start at least.

The bigger companies, like MacMillan Bloedel, B.C. Forest Products, Rayonier, Canadian Forest Products, Pacific Logging, Crown Zellerbach and the Tahsis Company have invited recreationists to share the forestlands on a multiple (integrated) use basis. They have provided road maps, erected signs declaring their multiple use policies, provided picnic and camping grounds.

Some recreationists set back the program by vandalism and theft, but in the main that has been kept at a minimum.

Recreationists, on the other hand, got access into the woods and saw the devastation that was being done by logging companies to the forestland environment.

There is a new awareness of the need to preserve the environment and the logging companies are sharing the concern, which in the past everyone seemed to ignore.

Logging companies have signified their willingness to

change their operations to fit in with environment and ecological protection.

All that is needed is a catalyst to bring all those concerned with the environment and land use together ... loggers, fish and wildlife biologists, park planners, naturalists, mining companies, hydro developers and anyone who seeks to use the land and water.

There must be land use planning — watershed by watershed.

With an expanding population and an ever-increasing amount of leisure time the demand for recreationland is exploding.

The logging areas are filling that demand on Vancouver Island. We are fortunate to have so much logging area. Nearly three-quarters of our Island is taken up in forestland that can provide recreation experiences and jobs forever. There will be no housing subdivisions, shopping centres and blacktop jungles in our forests.

What is needed now is a system of landscape logging to preserve the esthetic values of the forests, to protect fish and game habitat and still allow logging to continue and provide jobs. Mature timber stands that still exist must not be ravaged as in the past. Second growth timber now covering logged-over areas provides a new chance. We must not repeat the mistakes of the past.

This book tells about the recreation experiences already available in the forestlands of Vancouver Island.

NOTE:

Because some trips will be made just as easily from either direction, we have included reverse mileages in brackets on those trips for easy following. On many of the trips we have included the public roads leading to the logging areas.

Example:

Mile 2.6 (68.8) — Jacklin Road intersection

↑
MILEAGE FROM
"MILE ZERO"

"REVERSE MILEAGE"

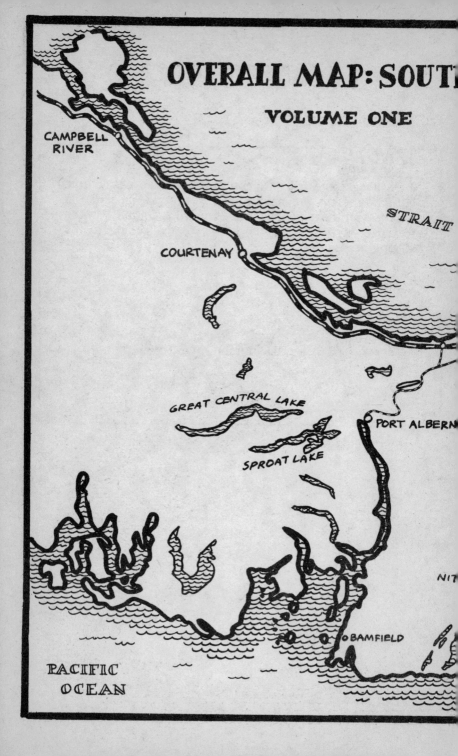

ERN VANCOUVER ISLAND

VICTORIA TO CAMPBELL RIVER

OF GEORGIA

SVILLE

NANAIMO

COWICHAN LAKE

DUNCAN

SHAWNIGAN LAKE

LAKE

VICTORIA

LANGFORD

PORT RENFREW

SOOKE

N

GULF ISLAND ADVENTURE
BY LAND AND SEA

For adventure that is a little different try visiting the beautiful Gulf Islands in the Gulf of Georgia.

They are ideal for bicycling, hiking or motoring and if you only have a small boat you can car-top or trail it to handy Gulf Island launching spots and live like rich yachtsmen on a 12-foot budget.

B.C. Ferries operate regular ferry trips to Salt Spring Island and also an Outer Islands service from the Swartz Bay terminal and a Crofton on Vancouver Island to Vesuvius on Salt Spring service. You can make a loop trip around Salt Spring Island, or if you wish you can make a Gulf Islands day cruise and take along a picnic lunch.

Pender islands are ideal for a camping-boating-motoring or cycling weekend.

You can camp at Prior Park provincial campground and hike its short mountain trails, launch your boat at the ramp at adjacent Browning Bay, cruise under the bridge and through the narrow channel between North and South Pender Islands, and tie up at the Bedwell Harbor marina alongside the palatial yachts and enjoy the facilities of the Bedwell Harbor Lodge.

You can even camp at Beaumont Marine Park in Bedwell Harbor, but you must reach it by boat.

You can enjoy the same luxuries as the big boaters, cruise and fish in the same Gulf Islands waters (except you make short trips ... and have a vacation weekend to satisfy a millionaire yachtsman.

The secret is to piggy-back or trailer your little boat and launch it where you can use it in comparatively sheltered waters. Then you have to pay more attention to tide, wind and other safety conditions than the boaters in bigger boats, but you can visit the same oyster and clam beaches, the same swimming holes and fish the same tide rips and points.

The still-unspoiled Pender islands ... North Pender, nine-by-five miles in area with less than 500 residents, and South Pender, 4 1/2 miles long by two miles wide, with less than 100 residents ... are ideal for boaters.

The two Penders are separated by Port Browning and Pender Harbor, with a narrow canal dug more than 50 years ago separating the two, which are connected by a narrow bridge over the canal.

FERRIES

VANCOUVER

GABRIOLA IS

NANAIMO

VALDES IS.

THETIS I

TSAWWASSEN

LADYSMITH

GALIANO IS.

FERRY

KUPER IS

MAYNE IS.

SATURNA IS.

SALTSPRING IS.

So. PENDER

DUNCAN. COWICHAN BAY

No. PENDER

ORCAS I.

SHAWNIGAN LAKE

FERRY

SWARTZ BAY

SIDNEY IS.

SAN JUAN IS.

ELK LAKE

VICTORIA

JORDAN RIVER

SOOKE

COLWOOD

FERRIES

SEATTLE

PORT ANGELES

Otter Bay, where the B.C. Ferry docks on North Pender, is an enjoyable 40-minute cruise from Swartz Bay.

There are more than 40 miles of road on the Pender islands and you can travel them all in a weekend.

From the ferry wharf it is 3.4 miles to Port Browning, the marina and 4.3 miles to Prior Park campground.

It is only a mile further on from the park to the bridge between the two islands.

There you will find a shingle beach spit where you can swim, picnic (no camping allowed) and launch your boats for free.

It is 10 miles from the park to Bedwell Harbor.

As a Customs port Bedwell Harbor is a bustling hive of industry.

We have made our Pender islands trips landlubber-marine weekends by taking a five-hour cruise around the Penders and Saturna Island in our 12-foot aluminum. The trip is feasible because you can duck into safety almost anywhere and you don't have to cross much open water. But you must have power. Those East Point tides are pretty fast and there is quite a fall and a strong tide in the canal between the Penders and in Boat Pass between Saturna and Samuel Islands, where there is sometimes a four-foot wall, which must be avoided in a small boat.

These government ferry schedules offer exciting adventures for island-hopping vacationists and excursionists.

Montague Harbor marine park on Galiano Island can be reached by car from the ferry docks ... and it is only a short drive, hike or bicycle ride.

There is a pretty good concrete slab launching ramp at Montague Harbor Park and it is within easy boating distance of Active Pass, but a little too far for Porlier Pass, unless you have fairly long range cruising power.

The park itself has two campgrounds, one for boaters and one for regular campers, and a series of interesting marine trails.

There is a magnificent shell beach and there are some good clam beds.

You could have a fine holiday without leaving Montague Harbor park, but there is plenty to see on the island and plenty of road to travel.

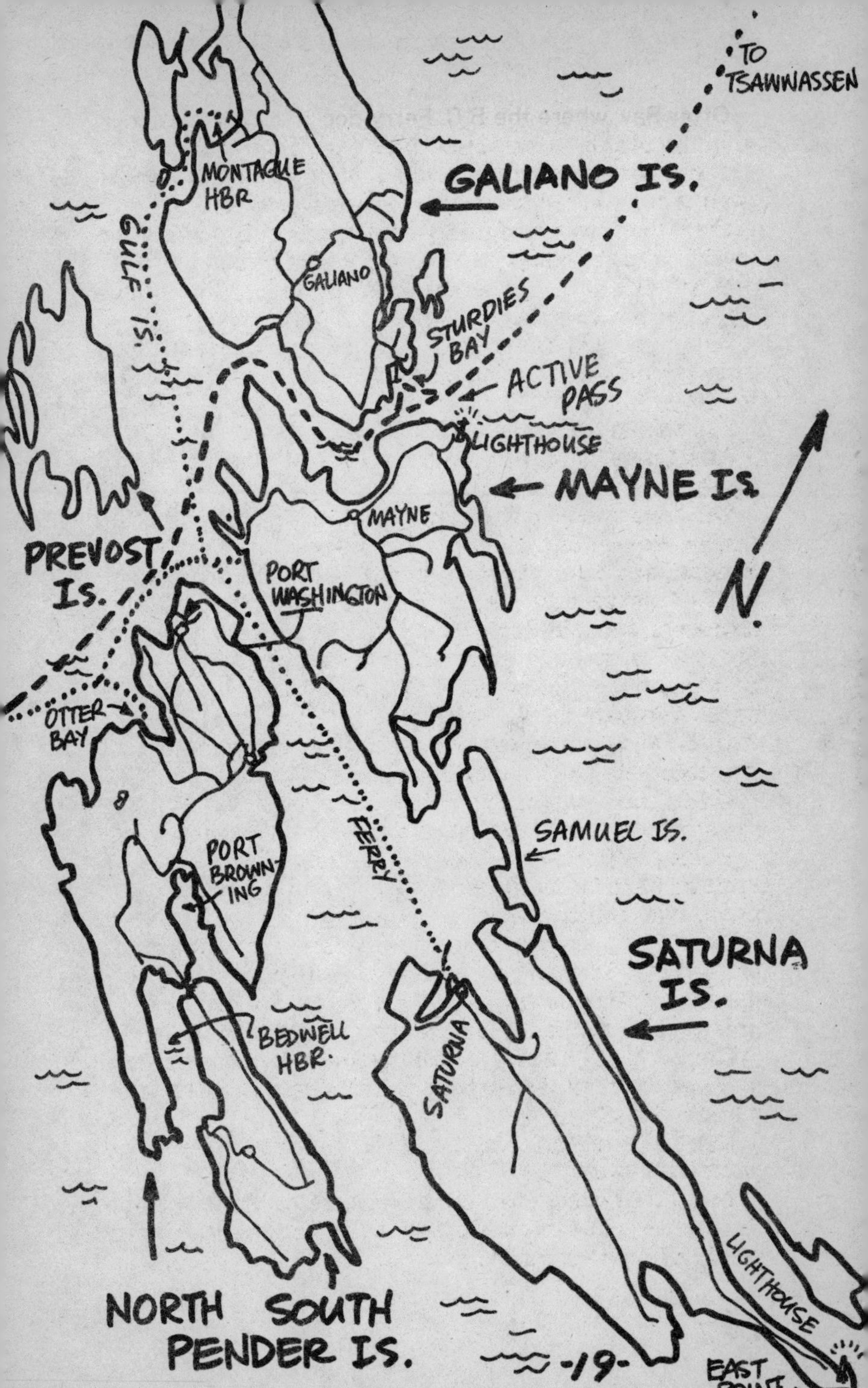

TO TSAWWASSEN

GALIANO IS.

MONTAGUE HBR

GULF IS.

GALIANO

STURDIES BAY

ACTIVE PASS

LIGHTHOUSE

MAYNE IS.

MAYNE

PREVOST IS.

PORT WASHINGTON

N.

OTTER BAY

SAMUEL IS.

PORT BROWN-ING

FERRY

SATURNA IS.

BEDWELL HBR.

SATURNA

LIGHTHOUSE

NORTH SOUTH PENDER IS.

EAST POINT

Spit on South Pender Island borders on canal between the two Pender Islands and is viewpoint for incessant marine traffic, as well as delightful picnicking spot.

Beautiful shell beach at Galiano Island's Montague Harbor Marine Park.

Active Pass viewed from Galiano Island's Bluffs Park.

The island is 16 miles long and two miles wide, possessing more shore line in relation to land area than any other of the Gulf Islands.

At the northern end of the island is Porlier Pass (between Galiano and Valdes), well known as The Gap, and there are lighthouses at both Race and Virago Points.

An unusual characteristic of lovely southern Galiano is its almost perpendicular bluffs, which afford a spectacular view of Active Pass. Covered with rock plants and colorful wild flowers, the bluffs are dominated by the oldest and largest trees on the island.

Take a drive along Active Pass Road for a wonderful view of the Pass and then turn off onto the Bluff Drive for an uphill, sometimes rough, drive to The Bluffs Park, which is really worthwhile visiting.

This makes a good spot for a picnic where you can relax on the grass and watch the ferries and pleasure boats compete in that busy narrow ribbon of water, where the tide sometimes boils so much that it is dangerous for even the bigger pleasure boats.

Then you can drive to Sturdies Bay on Active Pass, where the interconnecting mainland-Salt Spring ferry docks.

You can then drive the entire length of the island from south to north, taking in the golf course, the rod and gun club, Retreat Cove, Salishan Resort where you can camp in spring and fall, and rent cabins the year-round, Soanish Hills store, the boat ramp which enables boaters to launch for Porlier Pass fishing and on to Porlier Pass Marina.

On Salt Spring Island 1,200-acre Ruckle Farm at Beaver Point has been made into a class A provincial park and is a delightful place to visit.

The farm, with 4 1/2 miles of waterfront, was purchased in 1973 by the government and will be called Ruckle Provincial Park.

It is seven miles east of Fulford Harbor and has been used by campers and picnickers for many years, courtesy of the Ruckle family.

At the time of writing no park development had taken place, but there are cleared areas which campers use.

One or two spots have picnic tables and on the point itself is a big picnic table, suitable for a large group. School classes and outdoor groups often visit the park for study sessions along the several shale beaches, especially at low tides.

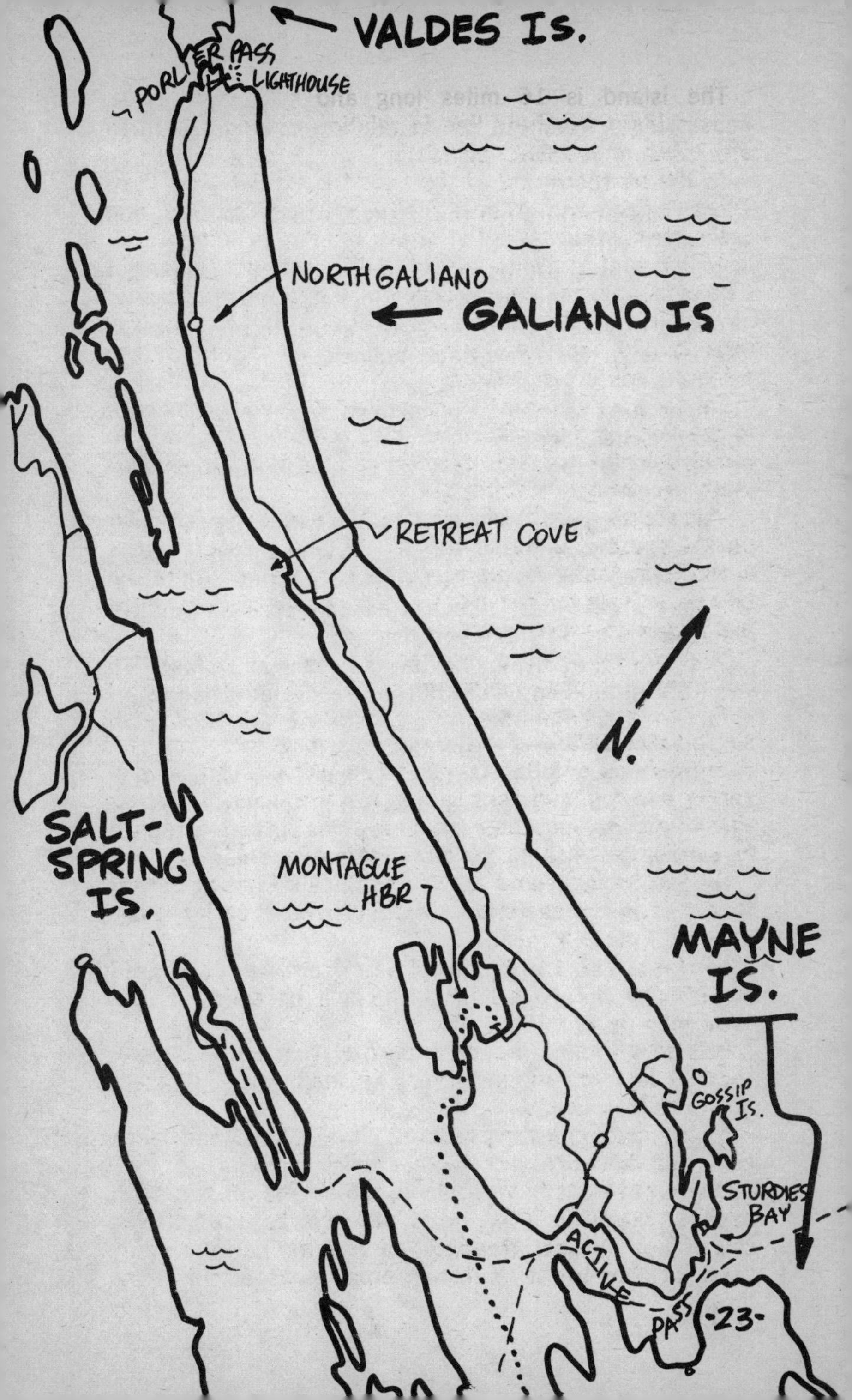

VALDES IS.

PORLIER PASS

LIGHTHOUSE

NORTH GALIANO

GALIANO IS

RETREAT COVE

N.

SALT-SPRING IS.

MONTAGUE HBR

MAYNE IS.

GOSSIP IS.

STURDIES BAY

ACTIVE PASS

-23-

The ferries and other marine traffic chugging back and forth ... into Otter Bay on Pender Island, off to Montague Harbor on Galiano Island, and so forth, a continuous moving seascape.

A trail leads through the rocky fields to Eleanor Point, the southeast tip of Salt Spring.

Salt Spring, the hub of the Gulf Islands, is a good place to visit, whether for a quick day trip, getting off the ferry at Fulford, driving around the sights and returning home via Vesuvius, or for a few days' holiday.

There is a government campsite at Mouat Park in Ganges and this is a nice place to stop, within easy walking distance of Ganges.

At Long Harbor the ferry takes off for the Vancouver-Islands service.

St. Mary Lake is a beautiful spot with bass and trout fishing and several resorts, including camping spots.

Mt. Maxwell is a favorite lookout spot and a park area.

There are at least 12 lakes on Salt Spring Island and most of them provide good fishing.

Best idea for a fishing holiday is to base at St. Mary. The Salt Spring Rod and Gun Club has provided small wharfs and boat launching roads at St. Mary, Weston, Stowell and Cusheon Lakes, which are the favorites.

Other lakes include Maxwell, which is the water supply for the Island; Bullocks, Stevens and Roberts, which are private lakes; Ford and Blackburn Lakes, where there is good evening fishing on the fly; Mitchell Lake and Allen Lake.

SOUTHEY PT.
GALIANO IS.
N
SALT SPRING ISLAND
SUNSET DR.
WALKER
HOOK ROAD
ST. MARY LAKE
WALKER HOOK
VESUVIUS BAY
TO CROFTON
SCOTT RD
GANGES
MOUAT PARK
TO VANCOUVER (TSAWWASSEN)
LONG HBR.
MAXWELL L.
ROBERTS L.
MITCHELL L.
FULFORD-GANGES RD.
CUSHEON LAKE
MAXWELL PARK
MAPLE BAY
BURGOYNE BAY
FORD L.
BEAVER PT ROAD
BEAVER POINT RUCKLE PARK
STOWELL L.
WESTON LAKE
FULFORD
MUSGRAVE
MT BRUCE PK.
ELEANOR Pt.
MT. TUAM
SWARTZ BAY
·25·

OUTDOOR MEALS
IN WINTER MONTHS

We like to eat outdoors as often as we can ... if eating in a comfortable motor home can really be called outdoors.

But, the difference between us and the "more rugged" outdoors persons is we eat "outdoors" the year round ... even in pelting rain, wind and snow.

If the weather is nice we go for a romp along a trail or a beach and Little Jo, the Labrador retriever just loves to come along, especially if there is some swimming, even if she has to break the ice or crash through ocean surf to get into the water.

Probably we do more lunch-time eating-out on short trips during winter and early spring ... and we have some favorite places. Of course all of them are pleasant the year-round, but we travel further and more often in the finer months.

If we are town shopping we often head up to the flagpole at the top of Beacon Hill Park for lunch. Sometimes we pick up fish and chips or a pork pie along the way. But more often Wife Taffy cooks up a lunch.

At the top of Beacon Hill the television reception is excellent, which is a comfort on a blustery and wet day.

We find Clover Point a nice spot for lunch, but sometimes a little smelly when the wind is blowing the wrong way.

The Breakwater is another nearby lunch spot and on a nice day a walk along the Breakwater can be a fine experience.

The top of Marine Drive on Gonzales Hill is another spot we sometimes stop for lunch. This affords a fine view of Trial Island and the waters on which I practically lived as a Foul (Gonzales) Bay youngster.

When we take grand-daughter Jennifer along we sometimes stop at Oak Bay Marina and if you can get a waterside parking spot out towards the breakwater it is a nice spot for lunch.

After lunch there is always Sealand and the performing killer whales, seals, porpoises to amuse Jennifer ... and we must admit us, too.

Mt. Tolmie park, reached from Mayfair Drive or Cedar Hill Cross Road has a number of enjoyable picnicking spots, plus several fabulous viewpoints.

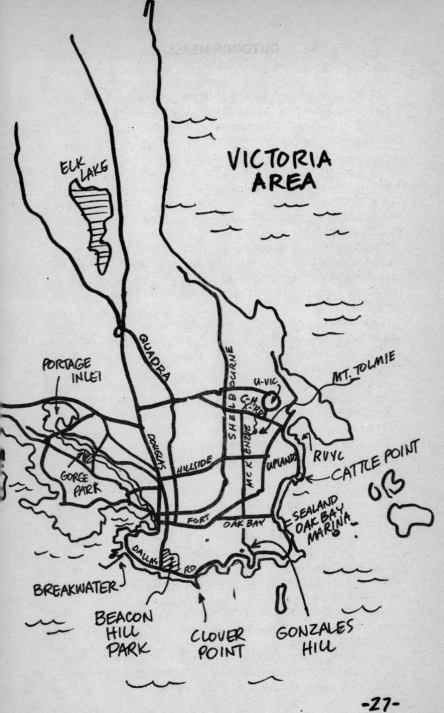

VICTORIA
AREA

ELK LAKE

PORTAGE INLET

QUADRA

SHELBOURNE

U-VIC

C.H. RD

MT. TOLMIE

GORGE PARK

DOUGLAS

HILLSIDE

MC KENZIE

UPLANDS

RVYC

CATTLE POINT

SEALAND
OAK BAY
MARINA

FORT

OAK BAY

DALLAS RD

BREAKWATER

BEACON
HILL
PARK

CLOVER
POINT

GONZALES
HILL

We have lunched at Cattle Point boat ramp in Uplands.

Island View Beach, off the Patricia Bay Highway, beyond Keating Cross Roads, is a favorite picnicking spot, an ideal place to launch our small boat, walk along the beach, and if we have enough time, to hike out to the point at Saanichton Spit and cast for salmon.

John Dean Park, off the East Saanich Road, is another handy spot for picnicking, has some interesting trails and is a particularly safe area for our dog and Chow Chow, our Siamese cat. They sort of regulate us, and we are always looking for a spot where they are not likely to be a nuisance to anyone else. Of course they are both very well trained ... and we always carry a shovel.

In Sidney there is a little beachside park just before the Sidney-Anacortes ferry terminal. It is a delightful spot to watch marine traffic and if you are lucky there will be sailboat races.

We don't go into the provincial parks very often in the summer after the gates go on, but in winter and early spring we spend a fair amount of time in the provincial parks which are always nice for a picnic.

McDonald Park, on the way to Swartz Bay ferry, is one of our favorites for lunch.

Back to the Esquimalt area, we have enjoyed picnics at Gorge Park, Kinver Beach boat ramp and Saxe Point.

Our very favorite lunching, or summer evening supper, spot is Esquimalt Lagoon, partly because it is so close to home, but even more because it is so delightful.

If you go out the Metchosin Road there are places to, lunch outdoors at Albert Head Lagoon, Witty's Lagoon (but you must carry your lunch to the beach) and at Taylor Beach.

In the Pedder Bay area, off the Rocky Point Road, is Matheson Lake Park. You can either lunch at the parking area and then walk to - and as far around as you wish - the lake, or you can carry your lunch a short distance to the lake and enjoy a waterside picnic. We do both.

Carry along the Becher Bay Road from Rocky Point and you will come to a wide parking area beside the road overlooking Becher Bay. This is a scenic place to stop, but not too safe for the dog and cat.

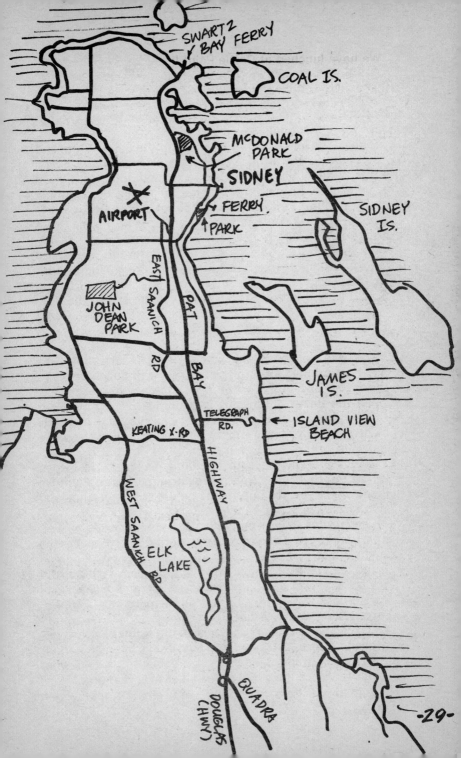

SWARTZ
BAY FERRY

COAL IS.

McDONALD
PARK

SIDNEY

AIRPORT

FERRY

PARK

SIDNEY IS.

EAST SAANICH RD

PAT BAY

JOHN DEAN PARK

JAMES IS.

TELEGRAPH RD.

ISLAND VIEW BEACH

KEATING X-RD

HIGHWAY

WEST SAANICH RD

ELK LAKE

QUADRA

DOUGLAS (HWY)

-29-

On the East Sooke Road, along the way to East Sooke Park, there is a place where you can pull off and lunch overlooking Anderson Cove.

Back on to Gillespie Road and half way along towards the Sooke Road is the bridge over Roche Cove. This is another favorite lunch spot for us.

Follow the Milnes Landing Road up the Sooke River and you come to the little picnicking area beside the Sooke River, with tables and toilets ... a good spot for a little steelheading in winter and some swimming in summer.

If you follow Kaltasin Road (just before the Sooke River bridge) you will come to a little park area at the mouth of Sooke River. This is now our clam digging spot. We dig clams, get crabs, and cook up a lunch from this little park.

Pass through Sooke Village and turn down Whiffen Spit Road for another nice picnicking area at the start of the Spit. It is an interesting hike to walk to the end of the Spit.

Just beyond the Butler log dump on the West Coast Road is a little beach with room for several picnickers.

Our own Gordon Beach, where we have our cabins, has plenty of parking area for picnickers, with good access to the beach and grand views of marine activity, especially when the heavy ocean surf is pounding.

At Tugwell Creek there is a nice picnicking spot, privately owned, but if you don't litter or carouse around you are welcome.

Then a short distance further along the West Coast Road is Flea Beach, French Beach provincial park, and Point No Point where you can buy afternoon tea at the tea shop and also stroll along the beach.

Then comes the Rayonier picnic ground at Jordan River, from where you can watch the surfers riding their boards in their wet suits.

Just 12 miles out the Island Highway from Victoria, and not too far from our Langford Lake home, is Goldstream Park where you can picnic in the campground in winter, early spring and late fall.

The regular picnic ground, beside the highway, is a lovely spot and the Goldstream Flats has always been one of our favorite lunch and supper spots, although it is somewhat restricted since the parks branch took over that area.

Goldstream Park features several hiking trails.

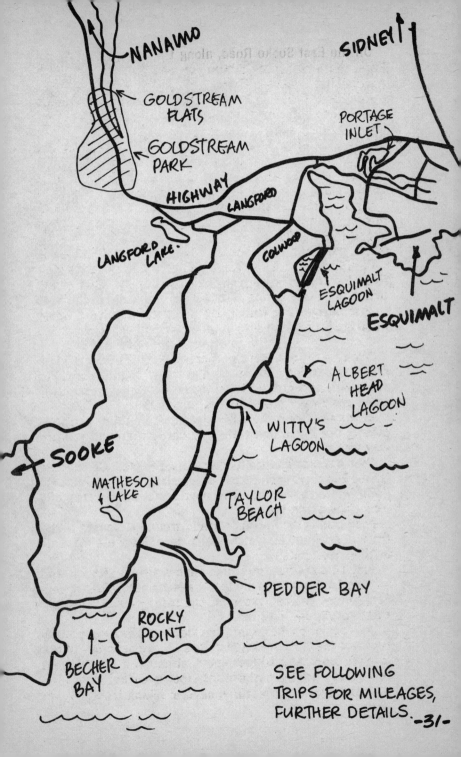

NANAIMO

SIDNEY

GOLDSTREAM
FLATS

GOLDSTREAM
PARK

PORTAGE
INLET

HIGHWAY

LANGFORD

COLWOOD

LANGFORD
LAKE

ESQUIMALT
LAGOON

ESQUIMALT

ALBERT
HEAD
LAGOON

WITTY'S
LAGOON

SOOKE

MATHESON
LAKE

TAYLOR
BEACH

PEDDER BAY

ROCKY
POINT

BECHER
BAY

SEE FOLLOWING
TRIPS FOR MILEAGES,
FURTHER DETAILS.

-31-

Then there is Spectacle Lake at the top of the Malahat, with a fine trail all around the lake, and a little further along the Malahat Drive, Bamberton Provincial Park with beachside picnic tables.

On our way up-Island we like to lunch right alongside the old highway at Mill Bay beach and also at the little picnic area across the road from Mason's Patio at top end of Shawnigan Lake.

Follow along the Port Renfrew Road from Shawnigan and you come to the Burnt Bridge over the Koksilah. That is another one of our favorite picnic spots.

Go a few miles further along the Port Renfrew Road and you will come to the turn for Weeks Lake. That is an early season fishing lake and a good place for a picnic.

Those are only a few places to picnic. There are scores more and we are continually searching for them.

(FOR 'BURNT BRIDGE', SEE PAGES 68 & 92)

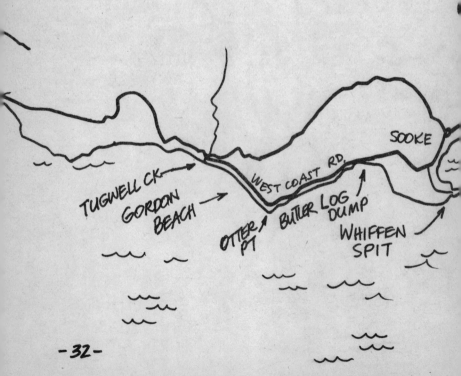

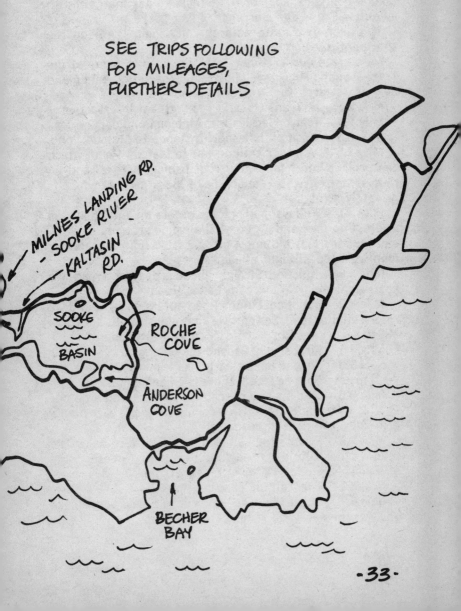

SEE TRIPS FOLLOWING
FOR MILEAGES,
FURTHER DETAILS

MILNES LANDING RD.
SOOKE RIVER
KALTASIN RD.

SOOKE
BASIN

ROCHE
COVE

ANDERSON
COVE

BECHER
BAY

HIGHLAND ROADS
CLOSE TO HOME

For driving adventure close to home you will find some interesting roads in the Highland district, although some you may find rather rough.

The trip we are about to describe doesn't need to be made in the loop we took. It can be made from several takeoff points for shorter trips to single destinations, with lakes like Pease and Durrance to fish, parks like Francis to visit, or for hikes into adjacent McKenzie Bight on the shores of Saanich Inlet.

We started our 27.4-mile loop trip close to home at the Trans-Canada Highway - Millstream Road intersection and headed towards the Western Speedway.

Mile Zero — Trans-Canada - Millstream intersection.

Mile 1.6 — Trail on left leads to Matson Pond dam.

Mile 2.3 — Trail on left short distance to Matson Pond.

Mile 2.5 — Another trail on left to Matson Pond, which can provide some fair kid's trout fishing. Across road on right is entrance to Teanook Lake (bass fishing) which is privately owned.

Mile 3.1 — Finlayson Arm Road enters on left. This is an interesting trip, ending up at the picnic grounds in Goldstream Park. It is a bumpy, but passable road. But for our loop we keep straight ahead.

Mile 3.6 — Junction. Straight ahead is dead-end road. We keep right along Millstream Lakes Road.

Mile 4.2 — Junction. Munns Road enters on right and we return on that road. For now we continue straight ahead on Millstream Lakes Road ... and it can be pretty rough.

Mile 4.6 — First sign of Second Lake on right.

Mile 5.0 — Second Lake clearly visible on right. There is a need to get public access to these Highland Lakes.

Mile 6.5 — Bad stretch of road, which required a detour last time we made drive. Then comes steep hill with plenty of bumpy boulders in roadway.

Mile 7.2 — Private road on right leads to Third Lake. The road we took continues rough and narrow down other side of hill. This section is really tough driving.

Mile 8.1 — Turn left to Pease Lake farm.

Mile 8.2 — Pease Lake. There is public access to this lake and it provides good fishing.

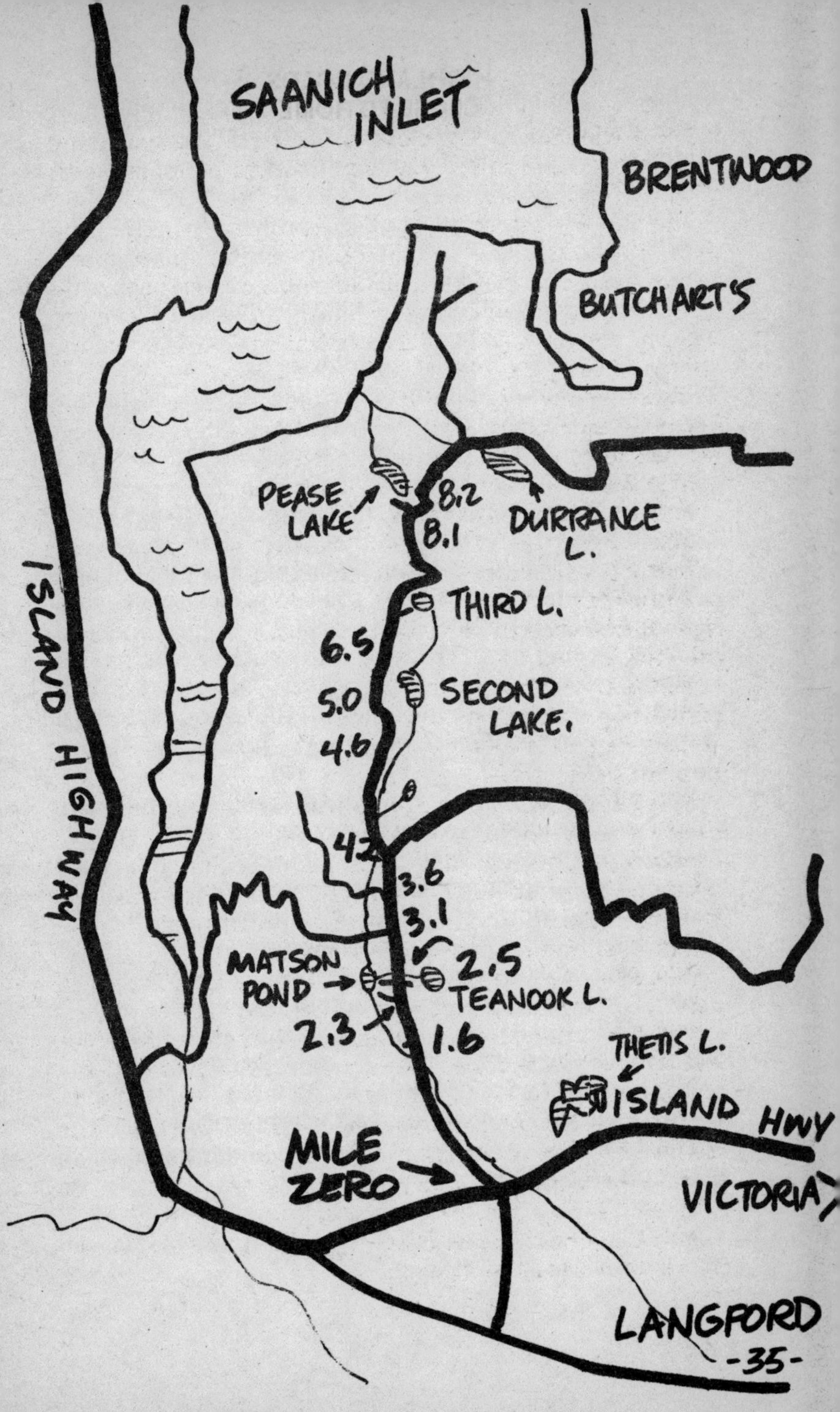

SAANICH INLET

BRENTWOOD

BUTCHART'S

PEASE LAKE

8.2
8.1

DURRANCE L.

THIRD L.

6.5

5.0

4.6

SECOND LAKE.

4.2

3.6

3.1

MATSON POND

2.5

TEANOOK L.

2.3

1.6

ISLAND HIGHWAY

THETIS L.

ISLAND HWY

MILE ZERO

VICTORIA

LANGFORD

-35-

Mile 8.9 — Junction. Left goes to Willis Point on Saanich Inlet for another interesting exploration trip.

Mile 9.3 — Durrance Lake, which provides bass and trout fishing and is regional parkland, but as yet there is not much parking space.

Mile 10.0 — Army check point for warning when Heals Range rife butts in use. Gravel road here.

Mile 10.8 — Second army check point and back to paved road.

Mile 11.7 — Wallace Drive intersection. You can turn right for Heals Range and West Saanich Road, or left for Brentwood. We go straight ahead.

Mile 12.1 — West Saanich Road. Left for Butchart Gardens and Brentwood. We turn right.

Mile 13.3— Wallace Drive joins West Saanich Road.

Mile 14.3 — Turn right for Prospect Lake.

Mile 14.8 — Prospect Lake swimming and picnic park.

Mile 15.2— Fire access road. You can launch small boats from this road, but there is no parking and road must be left clear at all times. Prospect, with limited access, gives up fine bass and trout fishing.

Mile 18.1— Munns Road on right. If you carry on straight ahead you come to Burnside Road. We turned right on to Munns.

Mile 18.5 — Francis Park. This is Freeman King's pet project and includes several lovely nature trails, a good place for a whole afternoon.

Mile 18.9— Centennial Trail, and then comes three sets of power lines which spoil the whole scenic countryside.

Mile 20.4 — Woodridge subdivision.

Mile 22.0 — Goodland Farm.

Mile 22.6— Fork Lake. Public access needed here.

Mile 23.2 — Junction with Millstream Lakes Road. We keep left to complete loop.

Mile 23.8 — Junction with Millstream Lakes Road and Millstream Road. We continue left the way we started.

Mile 27.4— Back at Trans-Canada - Millstream junction to complete loop trip.

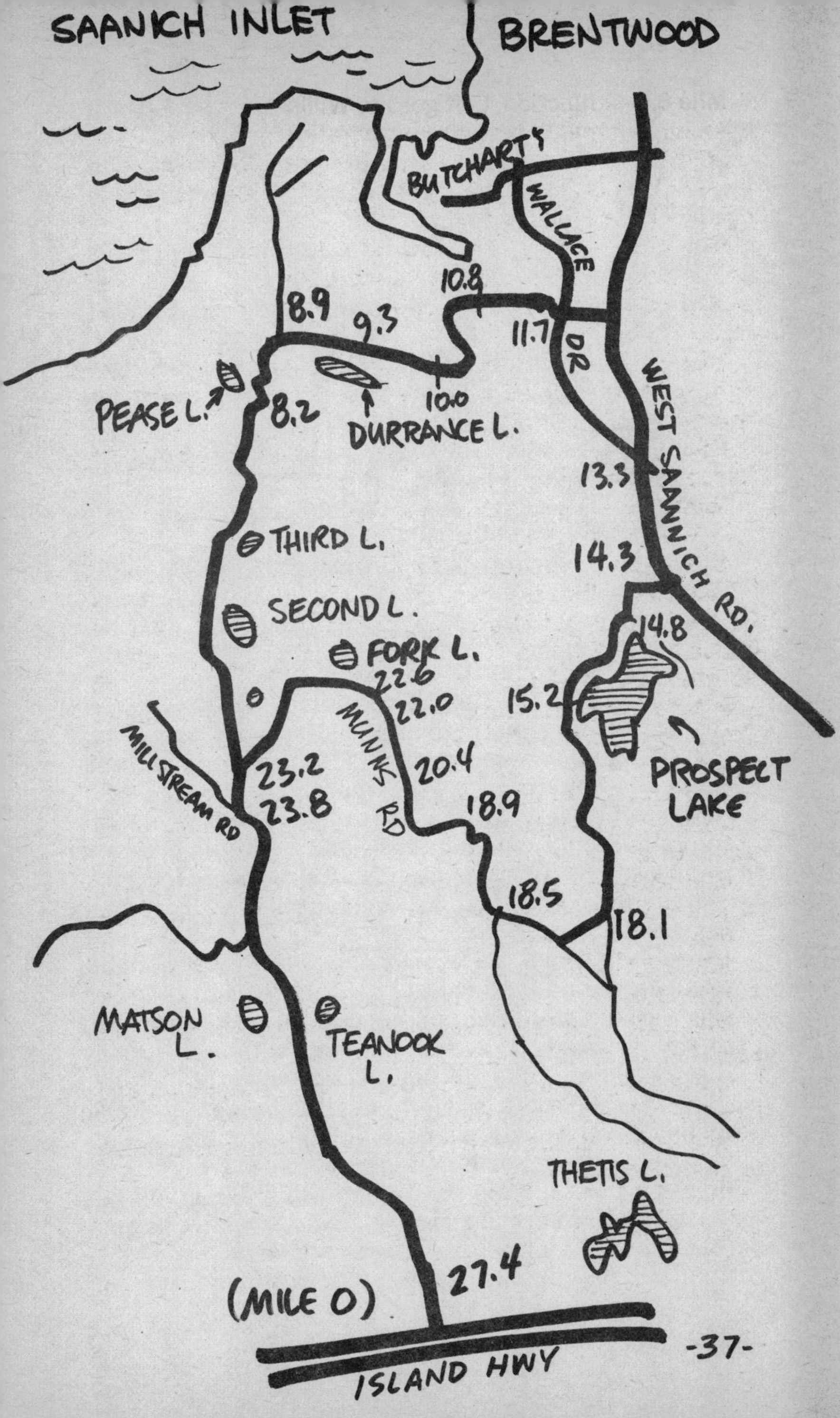

SAANICH INLET

BRENTWOOD

BUTCHART'S

WALLACE

8.9

9.3

10.8

11.7

DR.

PEASE L.

8.2

DURRANCE L.

10.0

WEST SAANICH RD.

13.3

14.3

THIRD L.

14.8

SECOND L.

FORK L.

22.6

22.0

15.2

PROSPECT LAKE

MILLSTREAM RD

MUNNS RD.

20.4

23.2

23.8

18.9

18.5

18.1

MATSON L.

TEANOOK L.

THETIS L.

(MILE 0)

27.4

-37-

ISLAND HWY

MacMILLAN BLOEDEL OPENS ROADS
FOR FULL TIME RECREATION USE

In October, 1973, MacMillan Bloedel initiated a new program which gives outdoor explorers and sportsmen hundreds and hundreds of miles of logging roads to travel 24 hours a day, seven days a week.

It opened its inactive logging roads in designated areas to the public on an all-hours basis and permitted overnght camping in the adjacent forests. It also embarked on a program to provide primitive camping facilities in many of the favorite spots.

Other companies have since followed MB's example although not on so grand and open a scale. Crown Zellerbach has stopped its permit system and has provided camping facilities at favorite locations within its logging claims, notable in the Nanaimo Lakes regions.

B.C. Forest Products which was the leader in public camping development has been quietly allowing full-time public access along some of its inactive logging roads.

In the major expansion of its land use program MB has also opened some main logging roads in active logging areas to provide full access, where road widths, and other conditions, permit safe, two-way traffic.

MB issued a new series of 17 maps, which show the 24-hour-a-day access routes in red ... and MB is really operating in the red.

The maps may be obtained from MB Community Relations Office, 401-3rd Avenue N., Port Alberni; or MB Community Relations Office, 55 Front Street, Nanaimo, or company division headquarters offices; or from tourist bureaus at Campbell River, Courtenay, Duncan, Nanaimo, Parksville, Port Alberni, Powell River, Qualicum and Squamish.

Practically all of the Shawnigan Division roads, reached from Island Highway at Duncan, turn west on road to Deerholme, four miles, are open at all times, and that includes the road to Wild Deer Lake where there is some excellent trout fishing.

The main line of the Chemainus Division in the Copper Canyon area is now open at all hours.

Northwest Bay Division has opened the access to the Boomerang Lake chain for all-hour travel, but all the rest of that division remains a weekends-only access proposition.

You can now drive through to Bamfield from Port Alberni at all hours, and also into the Nitinat Lake from Cowichan Lake, but you should wait for a radio-equipped control car to take you through from the Nitinat River Red Bridge to the Port Alberni - Bamfield Road at Franklin River camp.

In the Kennedy Lake Division the road along Maggie Lake to Toquart Bay is a fully open road and so is the short road into Kennedy Lake.

In the Sproat Lake Division most of the Ash River-Elsie Lake roads, reached from the bridge at the foot of Great Central Lake, are now open on a full-time basis ... and the roads have been signed to guide visitors through this complex-lake-studded system.

In the Menzies Bay Division you may now take the mainline road from Menzies Bay, through to Mohun Lake (and on to Morton) and further along to Brewster, up Brewster to Spirit, or on the west side of Brewster along the Memekay Main and the Salmon River to Kelsey Bay.

The Iron River road which gives some access to Oyster River fishing spots is open.

The Adam and Eve mainline roads are open.

Caution
Heavy Vehicles

OPEN TO PUBLIC TRAFFIC
DRIVE WITH EXTREME CARE
OBSERVE ALL SIGNS

YIELD TO LOGGING TRAFFIC

MacMillan Bloedel

Welcome

INACTIVE FOREST AREA
ROAD OPEN TO PUBLIC
AT ALL TIMES

PLEASE DRIVE CAREFULLY

MacMillan Bloedel

Active
Logging Area

PUBLIC MAY DRIVE HERE
ONLY BETWEEN:

5:00 P.M.–6:30 A.M. –WEEKDAYS

OPEN WEEKENDS AND HOLIDAYS
PLEASE DRIVE CAREFULLY

MacMillan Bloedel

As part of the expanded public access program MB erected new signs which detail the status of the road.

One sign reads: "Caution Heavy Vehicles. Open to public traffic. Drive with extreme care. Observe all signs. Yield to logging traffic."

Another reads: "Welcome. Inactive forest area. Road open to public at all times. Please drive carefully."

The other reads: "Active logging area. Public may drive here only between 5 p.m. and 6.30 a.m. - weekdays. Open weekends and holidays. Please drive carefully."

The expanded land-use plan of MB is to include pocket wilderness areas, experimental campsites, boat launching ramps, nature trails and ski runs.

During periods of high fire hazard, however, public access will be suspended.

New logging road to Nahmint skirts Alberni Inlet.

SOOKE—PORT RENFREW
VICTORIA'S PLAYGROUND

The Sooke - Port Renfrew area is the playground for Greater Victorians.

Within a few hours, or a day-long drive, outdoorsmen can find fine salmon fishing, beaches for swimming, clam digging, driftwooding, rockhounding, lakes for trout fishing,

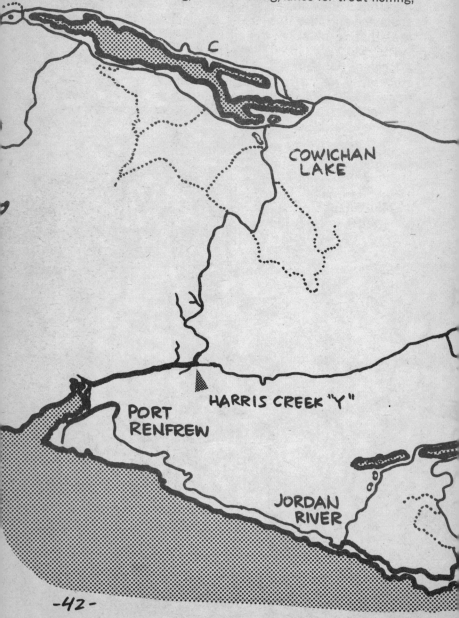

COWICHAN LAKE

HARRIS CREEK "Y"

PORT RENFREW

JORDAN RIVER

sandstone ledges that are uncovered at low tides to provide splendid inter-tidal zone exploring, forest trails for exploring, rivers for cutthroat trout and steelhead fishing, and hundreds of miles of logging roads to explore.

We will use Colwood Corner as starting point for our explorations.

The road from Colwood to Jordan River isn't a logging road, but it provides access to so many outdoor pleasure spots and entrance to so many logging roads in the Sooke area, that we must consider it a part of this book.

The road from Jordan River to Port Renfrew is no longer a logging road, but it is still used frequently by logging trucks and we advise travelling it during non-operating hours when practical. It is open to public at all hours, though there are several spots where we would not like to meet an on-coming logging truck.

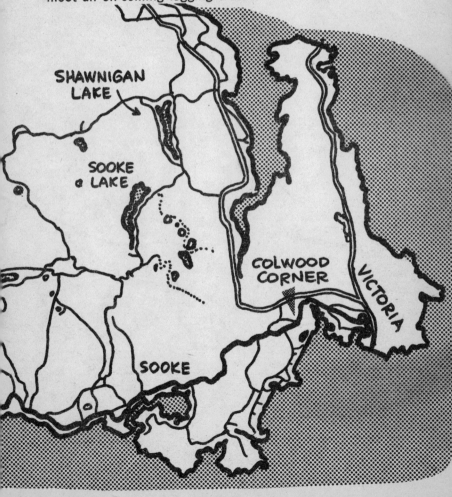

SOOKE — PORT RENFREW
VICTORIA'S PLAYGROUND

Mile zero (71.4) — Colwood Corner traffic lights.

Mile 1.5 (69.9) — Metchosin Road intersection, to Metchosin, Witty's Lagoon, Weir's Beach and alternative road to Rocky Point, Pedder Bay and Becher Bay.

Mile 2.6 (68.8) — Jacklin Road intersection. Alternative route connecting with Trans-Canada Highway.

Mile 3.1 (68.3) — Intersection with Happy Valley Road, which goes to South Vancouver Island Rangers, Pedder Bay and on to Becher Bay and alternative route to Metchosin and Weir's Beach.

Mile 5.4 (66.0) — Humpback Road, which goes along watershed to Goldstream Inn, Goldstream Park and Trans-Canada Highway.

Mile 8.6 (62.8) — Kangaroo Road, a connecting road which goes to Rocky Point Road, leading to Pedder Bay, Becher Bay, and to Metchosin and Happy Valley Roads.

Mile 8.9 (62.5) — Motorcycle headquarters. Beside Sooke highway at this point McKenzie Creek can be reached for kid's trout fishing.

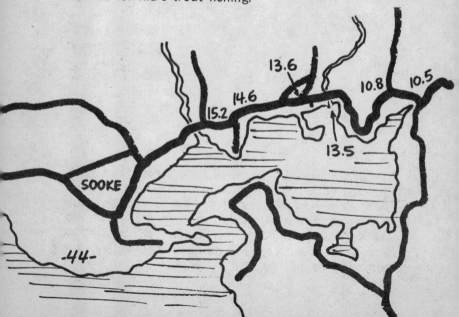

Mile 10.4 (61.0) — Gillespie Road. This leads to East Sooke regional park and Becher Bay fishing resorts — see mileage from Happy Valley junction and reverse them.

Mile 10.8 (60.6) — Glinz Lake Road to YM — Camp Thunderbird, and hiking and hunting areas beyond.

Mile 13.4 (58.0) — Stoney Creek, which affords a spectacular view of spawning chum salmon around Remembrance Day weekend. (Nov. 11.)

Mile 13.5 (57.9) — Sunny Shores Camp for camping, boat launching and boat rentals.

Mile 13.6 (57.8) — Harborview Road. Turn right for Grassie, Shields, Crabapple Lakes.

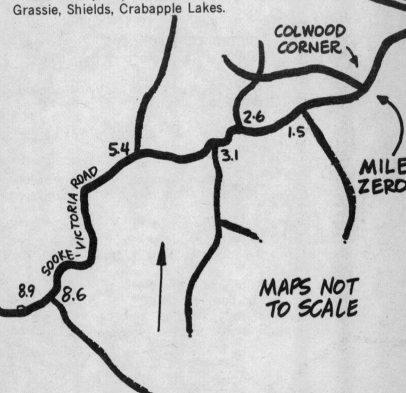

VICTORIA →

COLWOOD CORNER

2·6

1·5

5.4

3.1

SOOKE-VICTORIA ROAD

8.9

8.6

MILE ZERO

MAPS NOT TO SCALE

Mile 14.6 (56.8) — Kaltasin Road, which leads to Billing's (Jackson's) spit between inner and outer basins of Sooke Harbor for clam digging, shrimping (October to December in middle of basin), searun cutthroat fishing and crabbing.

Mile 15.2 (56.2) — Sooke River Road at Milnes Landing, leading to Sooke River Potholes, steelheading and swimming spots.

COLWOOD — JORDAN RIVER SIDE TRIPS
FOR BEACHES AND SALMON FISHING

Some of the best salmon fishing in the world is found in the Colwood to Jordan River waterfront areas and side roads lead to marinas and boat launching and rental spots.

They also lead to beaches for swimming, clam digging, and explorings as well as to a fabulous system of logging roads.

SIDE TRIP TO METCHOSIN

Mile Zero — Metchosin Road intersection at Mile 1.5 mark.

Mile 1.0 — Left, down Lagoon Road to Esquimalt Lagoon.

Mile 2.4 — Farhill Road, which leads to Albert Head Lagoon.

Mile 2.8 — Duke Road on left. Leads to Witty's Lagoon shores, but not good access.

Mile 3.6 — Other end of Duke Road.

Mile 4.8 — Witty's Lagoon Road, half a mile to beach access and lovely regional park, with sandy beach, lagoon and trail to falls.

Mile 5.2 — Metchosin intersection. Right turn for 3/10th mile leads to Happy Valley and Rocky Point Road junction to Pedder and Becher Bay. Straight ahead for Weir's Beach.

Mile 6.0 — Left turn for Taylor Beach.

Mile 6.7 — Fernie Farm for teas.

Mile 7.5 — Weir's Beach resort. Sandy beach, camping, boat launching for salmon fishing, swimming pool.

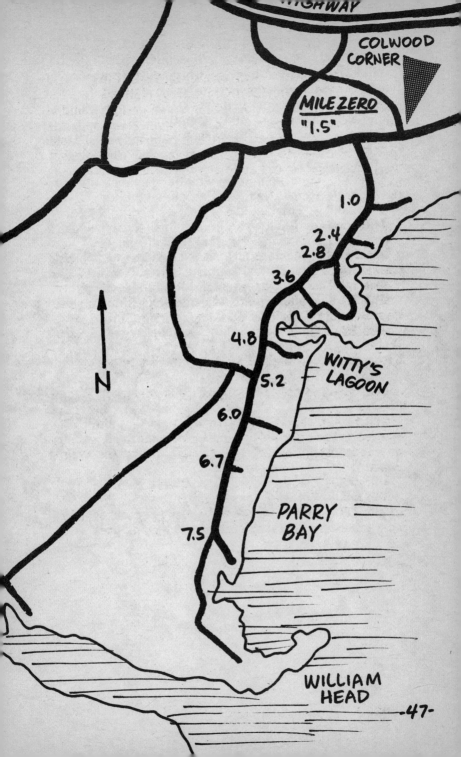

HIGHWAY

COLWOOD
CORNER

MILE ZERO
"1.5"

1.0

2.4
2.8

3.6

4.8

5.2

WITTY'S
LAGOON

6.0

6.7

PARRY
BAY

7.5

N

WILLIAM
HEAD

SIDE TRIP TO PEDDER, BECHER BAYS

Mile Zero— Happy Valley intersection at Mile 3.1 mark.

Mile 1.1 — Luxton Road, entrance to South Vancouver Island Rangers complex.

Mile 6.4 — Junction. Left for 3/10ths of mile to join Metchosin Road. Right for Pedder Bay, Becher Bay.

Mile 9.6 — Road to Matheson Lake provincial park on right. Good fishing, hiking trails. Road to Pedder Bay Marina salmon fishing waters, on left.

Mile 9.9 — Junction. Rocky Point arsenal on left. Keep straight ahead and right for Becher Bay.

Mile 10.1 — Enter Indian Reserve.

Mile 11.3 — Cheanuh Marina Indian boat launching ramp and campground, for Becher Bay fishing.

Mile 12.7 — Left turn for Pacific Lions Marina and boat launching at Becher Bay. Southeasterly entrance to East Sooke regional park beaches and hiking trails.

Mile 13.9— Junction with Gillespie Road. Straight ahead for East Sooke regional park hiking trails. Turn right for Sooke Road.

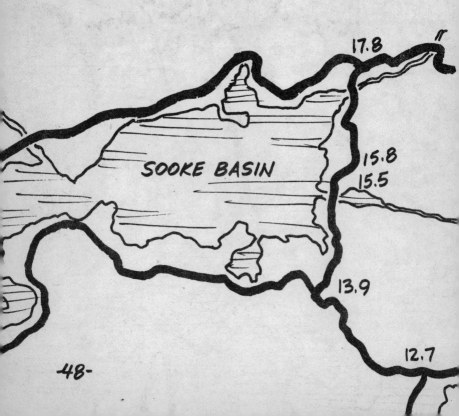

Mile 15.5 — Roche Cove bridge, a lovely spot for a picnic.

Mile 15.8 — Railway overpass. Hike along railway tracks for Matheson Lake.

Mile 17.8 — Junction with Sooke — West Coast Road at Mile 10.4.

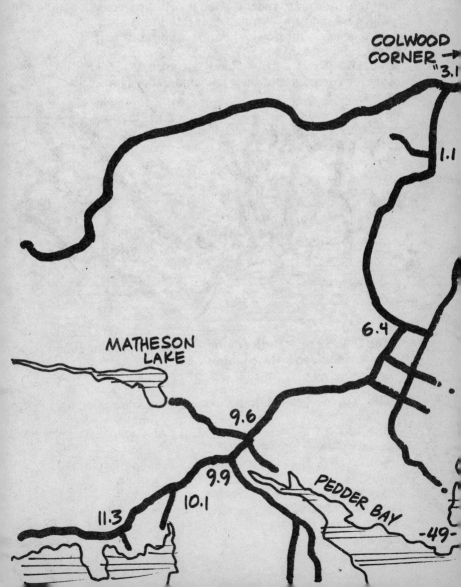

Mile 15.3 (56.1) — Sooke River bridge.

Mile 16.4 (55.0) — Sooke Village, and Otter Point road which leads to logging roads back of Sooke. **See separate chapter on Sooke logging road network.**

Mile 16.8 (54.6) — Sooke wharf and commercial fishboat tieup.

Mile 17.1 (54.3) — Sooke Harbor Marina for all-weather wharfage and boat launching for sports fishermen.

Mile 17.4 (54.0) — Whiffen Spit Road for beach hiking, clam digging, waterfowl shooting and cutthroat trout fishing from spit.

Mile 18.2 (53.2) — Ella Road entrance to Sooke Bay Resort for camping and boat launching and agate collecting on beach.

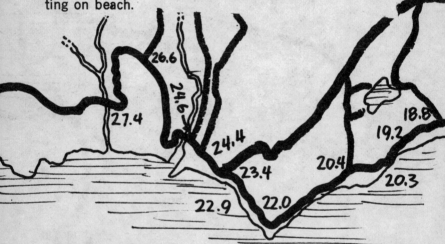

Mile 18.8 (52.6) — Butler dump, entrance to logging road network. (**see separate chapter**)

Mile 19.2 (52.2) — Beach picnic area.

Mile 20.3 (51.1) — Caravan Juan de Fuca for camping, boat launching.

Mile 20.4 (51.0) — Kemp Lake Road on right, to Kemp Lake and Otter Point Road.

Mile 22.0 (49.4) — Otter Point. Fish salmon by spinning from rocks.

Mile 22.9 (48.5) — Gordon Beach, first view of Pacific ocean surf. Limited boat launching for small boats and a favorite beach for rockhounds and driftwood collectors.

Mile 23.4 (48.0) — Right turn for Otter Point Road.

Mile 23.7 (47.7) — Tugwell Creek.

Mile 24.4 (47.0) Right on Anderson Road to Elder Logging Roads and to Ranger and Tugwell Lakes on road that connects with Butler Main Line.

Mile 24.6 (46.8) — Muir Creek. Entrance to logging road system for non-operating hour travel. (**See separate chapter on Sooke logging roads.**] Drop down bank up-

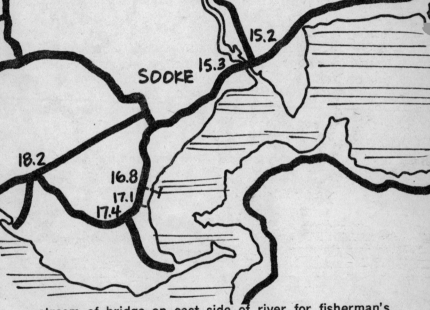

stream of bridge on east side of river for fisherman's footpath for short distance up river. Cross bridge and take west bank downstream for estuary cutthroat fishing. Walk along beach to Kirby Creek to see fossils.

Mile 26.6 (44.8) — Road on right leads into blueberry patch at top of Shirley Hill, for September picking.

Mile 27.4 (44.0) — Kirby Creek. This creek sometimes provides good steelhead and searun cutthroat fishing, but it is mostly on private property.

Mile 29.8 (41.6) — French Beach Park trail.

Mile 31.9 (39.5) — Point No Point tearoom and beach trails.

JORDAN RIVER TO PORT RENFREW
FOR HIKING TRAILS AND BEACHES

Once you leave Jordan River you are really on logging roads, although officially it is a public road into Port Renfrew.

Side trails lead to fabulous hiking areas like China Beach, Sombrio Beach and Botanical Beach. And in San Juan Bay at Port Renfrew you can meet the salmon as they enter Juan de Fuca Strait, as well as get into the big halibut when they are on the banks in May.

At top of hill before entering Jordan River and just before the mine road is Rayonier's east main which leads to some fine trout fishing a few miles in.

Mile 36.6 (34.8) — Jordan River bridge. Surfers ride waves in all seasons off Jordan River beach. In August there is often good fly fishing under the bridge for ocean perch, or porgies. Rayonier has provided picnic park at bridge. You now share the road with logging trucks — **BE CAREFUL.** The Jordan River - Port Renfrew Road is public and open at all hours.

Mile 39.2 (32.2) — Left for parking lot and trail to China Beach provincial park, a delight, sandy Pacific Beach.

Mile 40.3 (31.1) — Mystic Creek Bridge. A rough trail leads to beach.

Mile 49.9 (21.5) — Loss Creek. A delightful spot to stop for lunch. There is a small park and riverside trail downstream. Only small fish in this part of river.

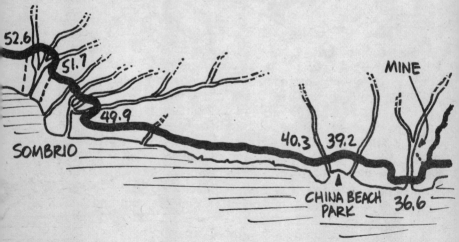

Mile 51.7 (19.7) — Logging road on left leads to parking lot for Sombrio Beach trail, keep straight ahead, don't take right or left turns. At parking lot look around for red tapes which lead way down steep trail to beach, 15 to 20 minutes down, longer up. This is the trail used by beach squatters and rather rugged for anyone not in good condition.

Mile 52.6 (18.8) — Small parking area on left at top of hill. There is an old Colonist sign tacked to pole on right. Park and walk back 10 or 15 yards and search in underbrush at side of road for old Outdoor Club marker which shows start of the first Sombrio Trail. Then look for red markers leading down steep bank. This can be quite a muddy trail, but not too hard hiking, half an hour to beach, three-quarters of an hour back up. Since first edition of this book Rayonier has rebuilt the trail for recreational use.

Sombrio is a more rugged Pacific ocean beach, with a cave and waterfall, and a spectacular sandstone shelf which is fascinating for inter-tidal zone explorers, as low tides uncover scores of tidal pools filled with marine life. If you haven't time to get to Botanical Beach at zero tides, try Sombrio.

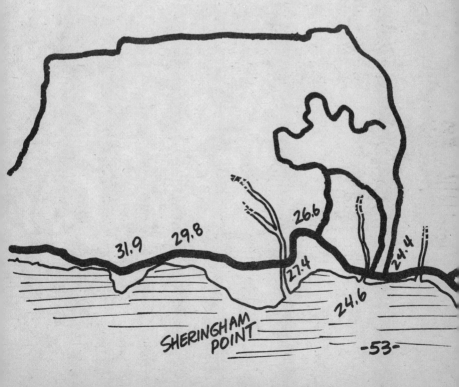

Surfing at Jordan River.

San Juan River steelhead. Left, Frank Baker, right Bob Davidson.

Rare trumpeter swans use slough beside logging road at
Port Renfrew as resting place.

China Beach on west coast is reached by trail just
beyond Jordan River.

Mile 60.6 (10.8) — Junction. Sharp right is old Bear Creek right-of-way and old Crossover Road, now abandoned. Sharp left on to pavement for main road to Port Renfrew.

Mile 62 (9.4) — Junction. Straight ahead for Port Renfrew. Botanical Beach turn is on left just before you reach Port Renfrew Hotel and docks. It is about three miles over rough (sometimes better to hike) logging road to beach (don't take right turn at junction on the way.) Botanical Beach has big sandstone shelf which provides a paradise of inter-tidal pools for marine students at extreme low tides.

You can gas up in Port Renfrew village before you get to dock.

Turn right for San Juan fun spots.

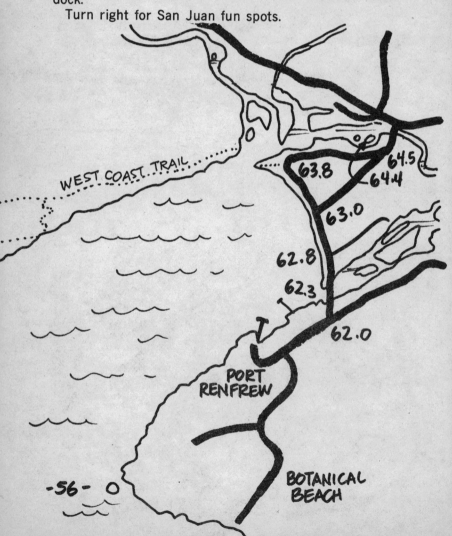

Mile 62.3 (9.1) — San Juan bridge. Turn left before bridge for launching ramp for San Juan Bay fishing, which provides chinooks in April, May, halibut in May, big coho and big chinooks in September and October.

Mile 62.8 (8.6) — Island Road. Turn right and follow road half a mile or so to first bridge over creek, for San Juan trout fishing pool on right.

Mile 63.0 (8.4) — New cutoff road on right, but keep straight ahead for scenic route.

Mile 63.8 (7.6) — Indian reserve picnicking and campground at mouth of San Juan River. Smelting from July until first heavy rains of fall, salmon fishing from beach and trout fishing at river mouth.

Across river is Gordon River and start of southern end of Pacific Rim West Coast Lifesaving Trail. Ferrying across river can be obtained from Indians, or by arrangement with Frank Elliott.

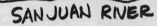

SAN JUAN RIVER

Mile 64.4 (7.0) — Elliott's Fishing Resort and cabins on San Juan River, a good base for Port Renfrew outdoor fun exploration.

Mile 64.5 (6.9) — New road rejoins old road.

FROM JORDAN -57- RIVER

Mile 64.8 (6.6) — Cross Deering bridge over north fork of San Juan River for junction, B.C. Forest Products Industrial site and restaurant on left, keep right for fun areas.

Mile 64.9 (6.5) — BCFP Deering riverside picnic ground. No camping, but picnic tables in the woods along the river. Swimming and fishing.

The road soon follows a roadside slough which is a backwater of the river and subject to tidal conditions. It is an excellent place to fish for searun cutthroat trout, especially in January and February, and is a resting stop for trumpeter swans and other waterfowl.

Mile 66.4 (5.0) — BCFP Fairy Lake campground on shores of Fairy Lake, where there is good trout fishing on fly and with bait and lures, and good swimming. Fairy Lake flows into the mainstream of the San Juan River and it is interesting to cruise out of the lake and into the river, but beware of river currents. This is the pullout spot for

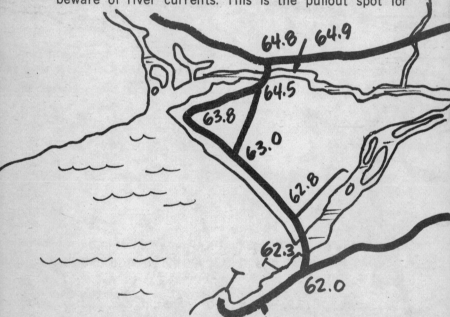

steelheaders or canoers who drift the river in boats from the black suspension bridge, about nine miles upstream ... a dangerous drift if you are not experienced at river-running. The campground is maintained in summer, but in winter is subject to flood conditions and you could be trapped overnight in several feet of water. Winter camping is without facilities and at your own risk.

Mile 69.3 (2.1) — Junction with Granite Creek mainline.

Mile 70.5 (.9) — Right for Crossover. Pool on San Juan River, about 2 1/2 miles, for no-facility overflow camping on river gravel bar in summer, picnicking and fishing. Part way in a trail on left leads to junction pool where Harris Creek and San Juan Rivers meet. Good steelheading and trout fishing water.

Mile 70.6 (.8) — Harris Creek bridge.

Mile 71.4 (zero) — The Y. Straight ahead and left on logging roads (access only in non-operating hours) to Cowichan Lake. Right on public road to Bear Creek, upper San Juan steelheading spots, and Koksilah - Shawnigan Lake roads, but this road is not always maintained and sometimes is impassible.

We will end our Colwood to Port Renfrew travels here and treat the Harris Creek Y as starting point for the other routes in or out of the Port Renfrew area.

HARRIS CREEK STEELHEAD POOLS
ALONG COWICHAN LAKE SHORTCUT

With the opening of the Hillcrest logging roads to Cowichan Lake Port Renfrew residents got a shortcut to the outside world, via Lake Cowichan.

Soon after leaving the Harris Creek Y steelheaders reach Mile 11 and Mile 12 on Harris Creek, some of the most productive year-round steelheading waters on all of Vancouver Island.

Mile zero (25.2) — Harris Creek Y. Keep left up hill.

Mile 1.1 (24.1) - Lizard Lake on right. Small campground. Trout fishing. This lake contains so much tiny crustacean food it is sometimes difficult to take fish, but it has been known to produce very big rainbows and is heavily stocked.

Mile 3.1 (22.1) — This is Mile 11. Look over bank on the left and you will find path which leads steeply down to the top of the Mile 11 Canyon Pool, which holds steelhead throughout the entire year. Further downstream another path leads to the lower pool, which can also be reached by a treacherous path between the two pools.

Mile 4.2 (21.0) — Path through the bush leads to Mile 12 steelheading spots, a corner pool, a series of runs, a productive bar and around the river upstream to the Canyon Bridge pools, where steelhead can often be seen below the bridge.

There is another fishing spot halfway between Mile 11 and Mile 12.

Mile 4.7 (20.5) — Canyon bridge. You can fish the downstream pool from the rocks below the bridge.

Just over the bridge, logging road on left is Hemmingsen Creek Mainline and there are steelhead to be taken in Hemmingsen Creek, but keep straight ahead for Cowichan.

Mile 6.5 (18.7) — Abandoned Harris Creek camp, with nothing left but a giant spruce designated as a point of interest. There is steelheading water along the road all the way from the Canyon Bridge to the old camp and just above the old camp is the old Swimming Hole Pool, which can be productive.

FROM PORT RENFREW

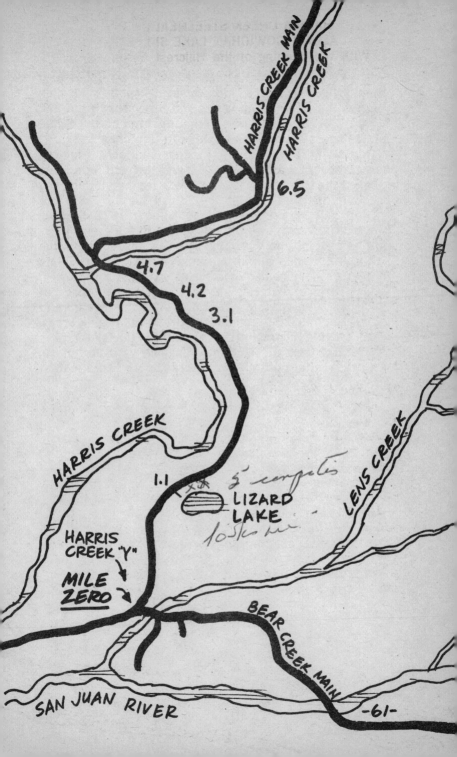

HARRIS CREEK MAIN

HARRIS CREEK

6.5

4.7

4.2

3.1

HARRIS CREEK

LENS CREEK

1.1

5 campsites

LIZARD LAKE

10 km wi

HARRIS CREEK "Y"

MILE ZERO

BEAR CREEK MAIN

SAN JUAN RIVER

-61-

Mile 11.6 (13.6) — The road follows Harris Creek past some lovely swimming and picnicking spots, and then reaches the intersection where you turn sharp right and leave BCFP Maquinna Tree Farm and enter through gate into Hillcrest country, and across to Cowichan Lake.

This is where travellers get a shameful look at logging desecration of past years. Cut and get out operators ravaged the trees for miles and miles, leaving nothing but bare mountainsides as far as you can see.

These hills were replanted in 1964 and in 1973 when we drove through them we were delighted to see green trees dotting the hillside. But the soil has eroded from the hilltops and these will likely remain barren and desolate forever, a damaging denunciation of logging of the past.

Just before entering McKenzie Logging yard at Cowichan Lake, roads on the left, around the Mile 23 and 24 marks enter 16 Creek and 19 Creek old logging areas, which provide grouse and deer shooting in the fall.

Mile 25.2 (zero) — McKenzie Logging yard and office, where you enter on to Cowichan Lake South Shore road at Mesachie Lake.

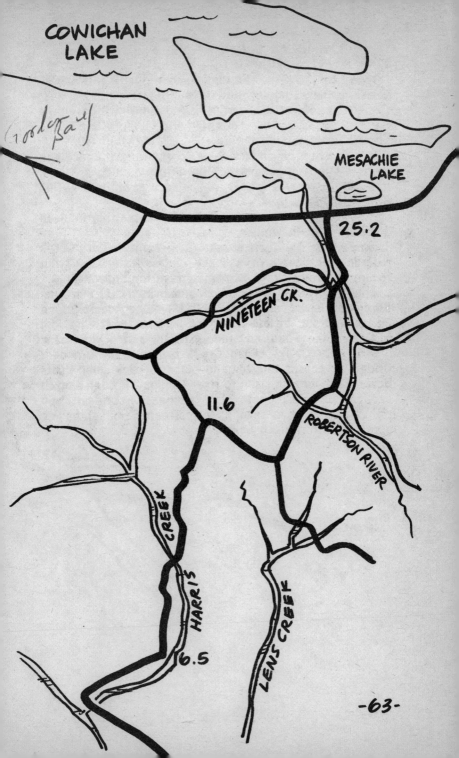

COWICHAN
LAKE

Goodgau?

MESACHIE
LAKE

25.2

NINETEEN CK.

11.6

ROBERTSON RIVER

CREEK

HARRIS

LENS CREEK

6.5

BEAR CREEK — SHAWNIGAN
RUGGED BUT ENTICING

In winter logging road travellers might find the Bear Creek to Shawnigan logging roads impassable beyond Bear Creek, but before the Bear Creek bridge they will reach the San Juan River campground and upper San Juan steelheading pools.

If they can go beyond the Bear Creek bridge they will find more steelheading pools, a rare wild rhododendron patch and fish-happy Weeks Lake, to say nothing of the beautiful Koksilah River.

Mile Zero (39.1) — Harris Creek Y. Keep straight ahead and right for Shawnigan Lake.

Mile 2.5 (36.6) — Left, about 2/10ths mile up Lens Creek mainline for right turn to short road to Pixie Lake, trout fishing and picnicking. Straight ahead for Shawnigan.

Mile 4.2 (34.9) — Black suspension bridge over San Juan River and B. C. Forest Products developed campground and picnic spot. We launch boats here for downstream float to Fairy Lake. Fishing water upstream and downstream.

Mile 6.5 (32.6) — Allan Creek bridge. Left turn over bridge for access to river and place to pack small boats down steep logging slash to river for float through canyon sections of San Juan to black suspension bridge. Keep right along new bypass loop for upstream San Juan fishing spots and Shawnigan Lake.

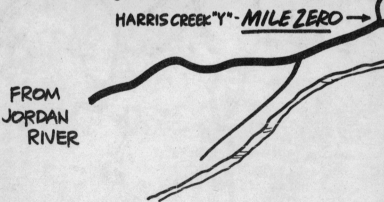

HARRIS CREEK "Y" - *MILE ZERO* →

FROM
JORDAN
RIVER

Mile 11.4 (27.7) — Bear Creek bridge. Park car at turning just before coming to bridge and hike through slash on left to find steep zig-zag path to what is known as the Bear Creek Meat Hole, for some fine steelheading water.

Often in winter and early spring you can't get beyond the Bear Creek bridge because of bad road conditions and snow on the road through timberlands ahead.

BCFP can't get their road graders over the bridge. But the company plans a new 3 1/2 mile bypass loop that will eliminate the bridge. It will start on the Shawnigan Lake side of the Bear Creek bridge and rejoin the existing road

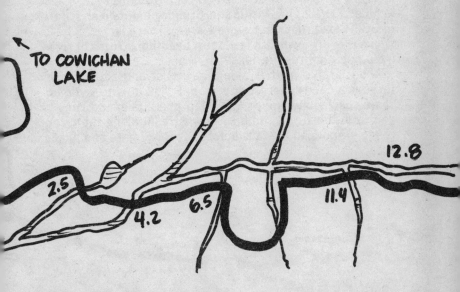

before the Allan Creek bridge. That will mean these mileages will be out somewhat, but they can be followed to the Bear Creek area from Shawnigan side and to Allan Creek from the Harris Creek Y.

Mile 12.8 (26.3) — Just 3/10ths mile beyond forest plantation signs, noting 1,300 acres of new forest planted from 1951 to 1958, take left turn down side road for 1/10ths mile and park in clearing at top of hill. Then walk down slate path to old foot suspension bridge (now removed). Trails lead steeply down to fishing water below.

Mile 13.3 (25.8) — Take overgrown road, sharp left and drive or walk through tunnel of willows and alder for about half mile to second blown trestle and good steelhead pools below.

Mile 15.5 (23.6) — Entrance to first blown trestle pools. If you haven't been there in recent years, it has changed. There is a washout and sort of gravel pit where you can park. Climb up the bank. There is a sort of trail on right. — look down and you will see an overgrown logging railroad grade. Follow that to old trestle and hike down steeply under trestle for some lovely steelheading water and canyon pools.

Then comes the curved suspension bridge which is always a thrill ride for the new travellers on this road.

Mile 17.0 (22.1) — Picnic site, drinking fountain and start of BCFP road (back to Renfrew area). There is a trail here which is overgrown, but leads to a beautiful stretch of river including picturesque falls.

About a mile further along, in timber and alder grove, there is a culvert across the road. Follow this to river for some spectacular upper San Juan pools, falls and runs ... and from these you can hike downstream along the river, rough in spots, to the falls before the BCFP gate and picnic area.

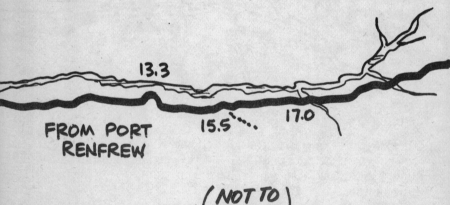

13.3

FROM PORT RENFREW

15.5   17.0

(NOT TO SCALE)

Mile 23.0 (16.1) — On the left you will see a one-acre clump of trees left in the logging slash. If you walk to this in June you will find a rare patch of wild rhododendrons which has been preserved by BCFP as a pocket park of interest.

Mile 24.0 (15.1) — Junction. Turn right for 3.2 miles to Weeks Lake and on to the Sooke logging network. This is the Mile 27.1 mark on the trip from Butler's log dump to Weeks Lake.

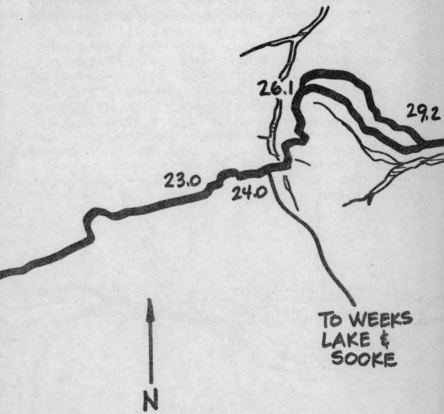

Mile 26.1 (13.0) — Junction with BCFP logging road. Right on to logging road during non operational hours for faster, shorter and better road. But because the Bear Creek - Shawnigan Road is a public road, open at all hours, we take rougher public road up and down steep hill.

At times we have found the government road impassable in early season.

Mile 29.2 (9.9) — Junction with logging road on right. We keep straight ahead on public road, down hill to old Kapoor and follow Koksilah River.

Mile 30.4 (8.7) — Lovely corner pool and provincial parks reserve on left. A cable bridge crosses the river at a good steelheading pool. If you want to see more of Koksilah River don't keep right at next junction, which is logging road which meets main road further along.

Mile 33.1 (6.0) — Junction. Left goes over Koksilah's Burnt Bridge. Keep right over bridge for Eagle Heights area. Left over bridge goes short distance to fine upstream riverside picnicking and camping areas. At times, often in April, there can be some steelheading in pools below bridge. Keep straight ahead at junction for Shawnigan.

Mile 39.1 (Mile Zero) — Junction. Right for Shawnigan's West Arm road for six miles to Shawnigan Cutoff Road and another 3.7 miles to 17-Mile Hill on Island highway. Straight ahead for Shawnigan Lake, Cobble Hill and Mill Bay.

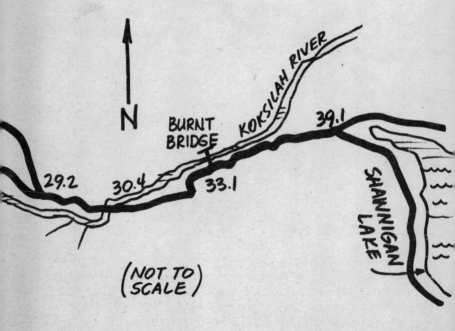

Wild rhododendrons bloom in preserved timber patch near Weeks Lake. Viewing time is June.

Years ago an unnamed logger dumped a few cutthroat trout in this lake at the 10 1/2 -Mile mark of the Butler Logging Road. Anglers still take some fish from it.

SOOKE LOGGING ROADS GIVE
ACCESS TO 230 SQUARE MILES

North and west of Sooke, between the West Coast Road and the Shawnigan Lake - Bear Creek Road there is a spider web-like system of logging roads serving 10 different logging companies and providing access to 230 square miles of recreation and logging land.

Further west in the Jordan River area Rayonier logging roads link up with this network and in addition Rayonier spurs provide short access to many more miles.

The Sooke Combined Fire Organization provides sportsman's guide maps for this region.

Access into this vast Sooke - Muir Mountain - Survey Mountain playland is from several points — through the Pacific Logging roads off Otter Point Road at the 2.2 mile mark; through the Butler logging road, off the Sooke West Coast Road at the 18.8 mile mark, or further along the same Butler logging road at the 3.2 mile mark on the Otter Point Road; through old Elder logging roads at the 24.4 mark; through Malloch and Moseley road at Muir Creek at the 24.6 mile mark on the West Coast Road; or from the Rayonier mainline just before entering Jordan River, although access on this road is not always allowed because of active logging.

You can also enter the Sooke logging road network from the Shawnigan Lake Cutoff and up the Leechtown Road along the waterboard's Sooke Lake, or from the Weeks Lake Road which you enter from the Shawnigan - Bear Creek - Port Renfrew Road at the mile 24 mark.

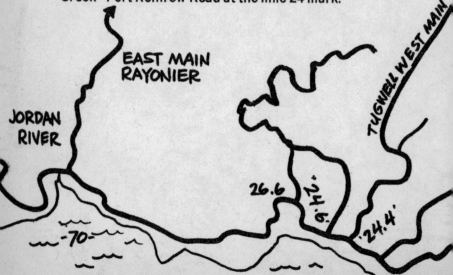

WEEK LAKE

EAST MAIN RAYONIER

JORDAN RIVER

TUGWELL WEST MAIN

26.6   24.6   24.4

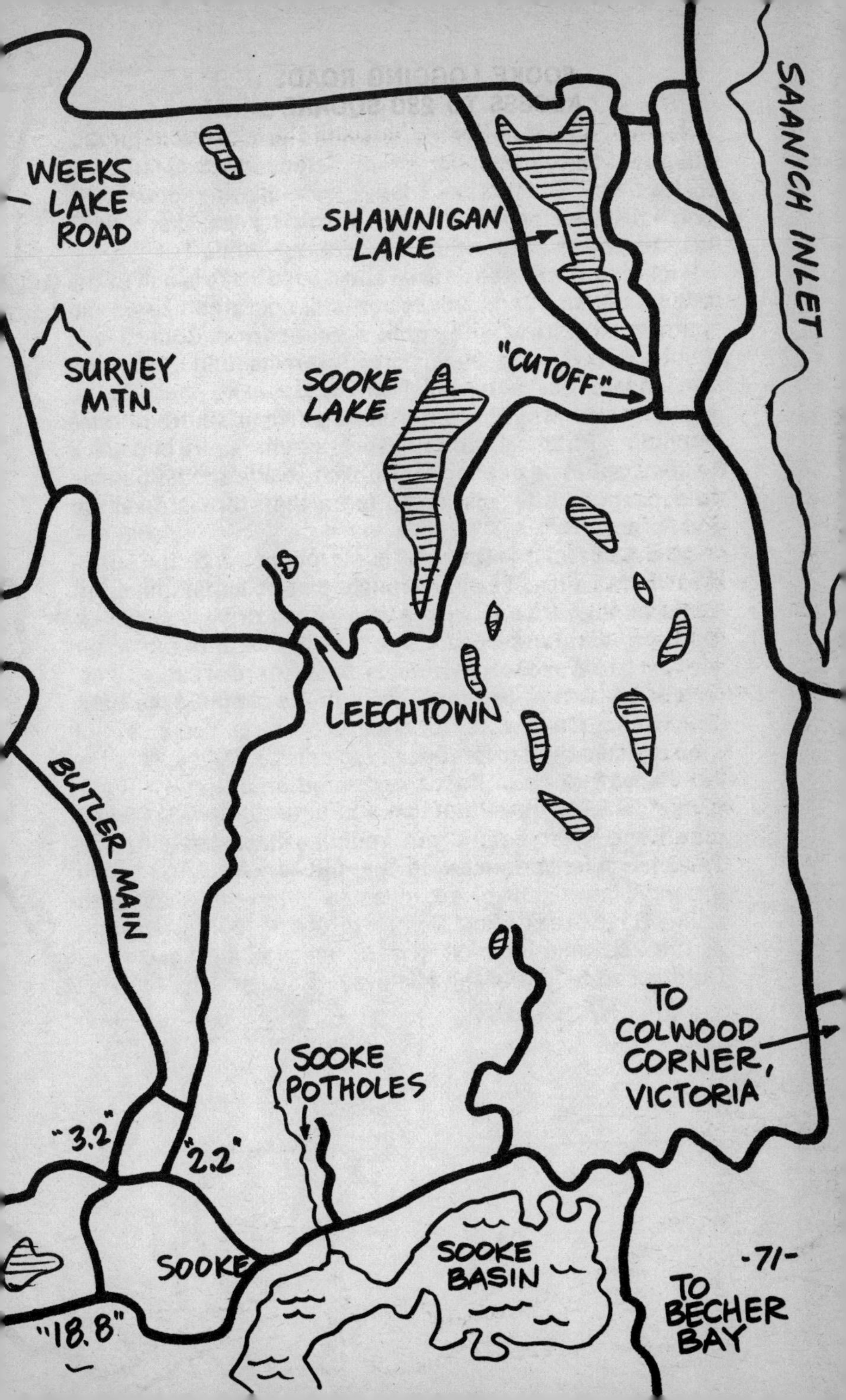

WEEKS
LAKE
ROAD

SHAWNIGAN
LAKE

SAANICH INLET

SURVEY
MTN.

SOOKE
LAKE

"CUTOFF"

LEECHTOWN

BUTLER MAIN

TO
COLWOOD
CORNER,
VICTORIA

SOOKE
POTHOLES

"3.2"

"2.2"

SOOKE

SOOKE
BASIN

-71-

TO
BECHER
BAY

"18.8"

Mile 12.8 (10.1) — Waterboard road on right, which will likely be locked. This road provides good access for 2.2 miles, for turn on left for short distance to Council Lake (bridge on Council Lake road, is now blown, so walk). A short distance beyond Council turning, keep sharp right, just before closed watershed gate, for Wolfe Lake.

This closed watershed area and Council lake is one of the last places on Vancouver Island still operated like an old feudal land system, with public access barred. Council lake is privately owned by logging interests and since the waterboard has a tunnel from Sooke Lake there is no logical reason why the waterboard's five or six trout lakes (including Butchart, Lubbe, Goldstream, Mavis and Jack Lakes) cannot be opened for public use. We should be able to expect some legislation to force these areas open for public use.

Mile 13.8 (9.1) — On right is old public road to Council and Wolfe Lakes. It is very rough, almost impassable, but some people drive it with a four-wheel drive vehicles. It connects with waterboard road before closed gate near entrance to Wolfe which is not in waterboard area.

Mile 14 (8.9) — Enter restricted area along Sooke Lake which is source of water for Greater Victoria. You must not stop or leave the car for next seven miles.

Mile 20.9 (2.0) — Leave restricted area.

Mile 22.9 (zero) — Junction and enter on to Shawnigan cutoff road just before you could make a left turn for 2/10ths mile and follow along public West Arm Road around Shawnigan for six miles to enter the Shawnigan Lake - Bear Creek - Port Renfrew Road. If you turned right at the 22.9 mile junction it is 3.7 miles along Shawnigan Cutoff road to join Island Highway at Seventeen Mile Hill.

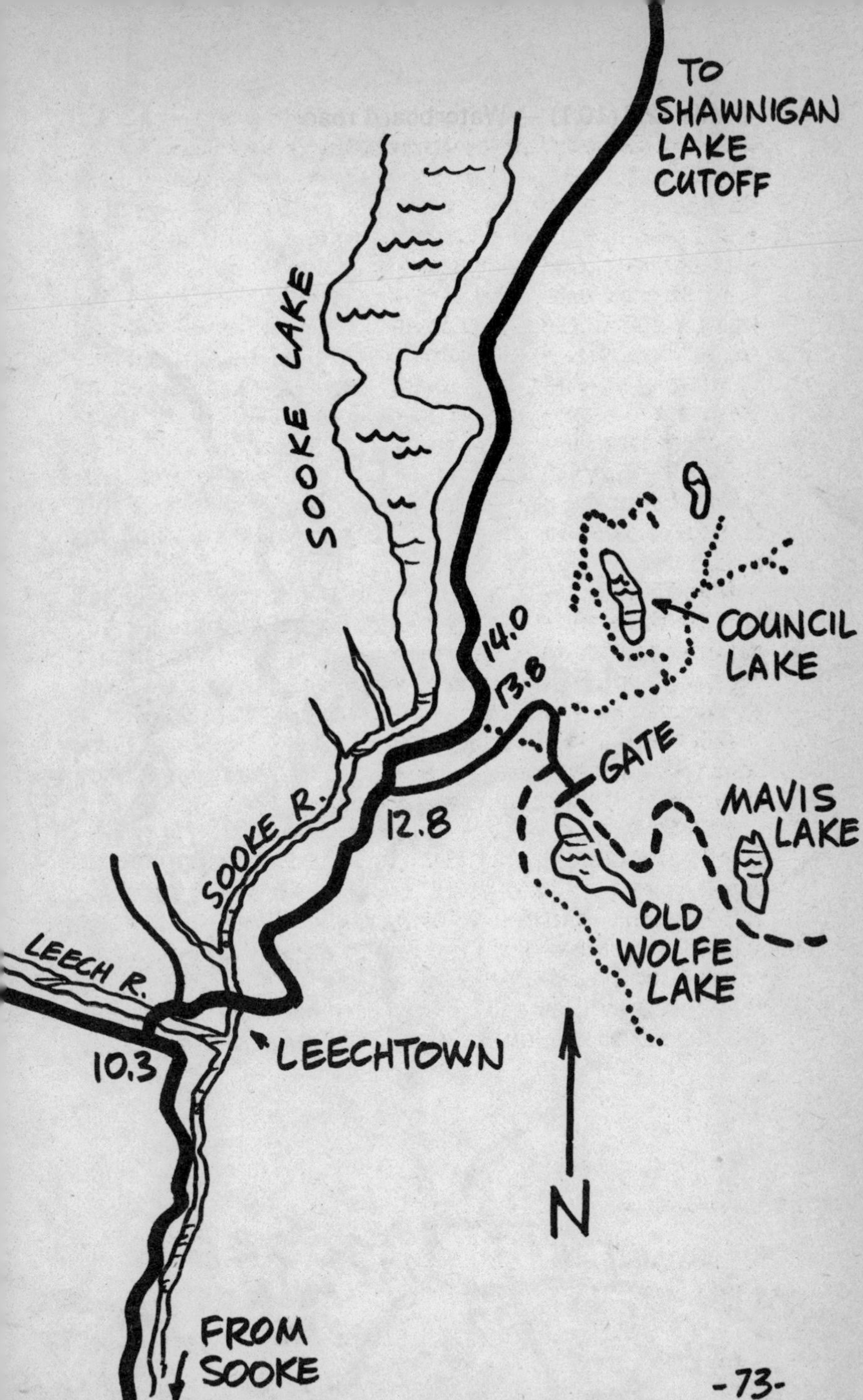

TO
SHAWNIGAN
LAKE
CUTOFF

SOOKE LAKE

COUNCIL
LAKE

14.0

13.8

GATE

MAVIS
LAKE

SOOKE R.

12.8

OLD
WOLFE
LAKE

LEECH R.

N

10.3

LEECHTOWN

FROM
SOOKE

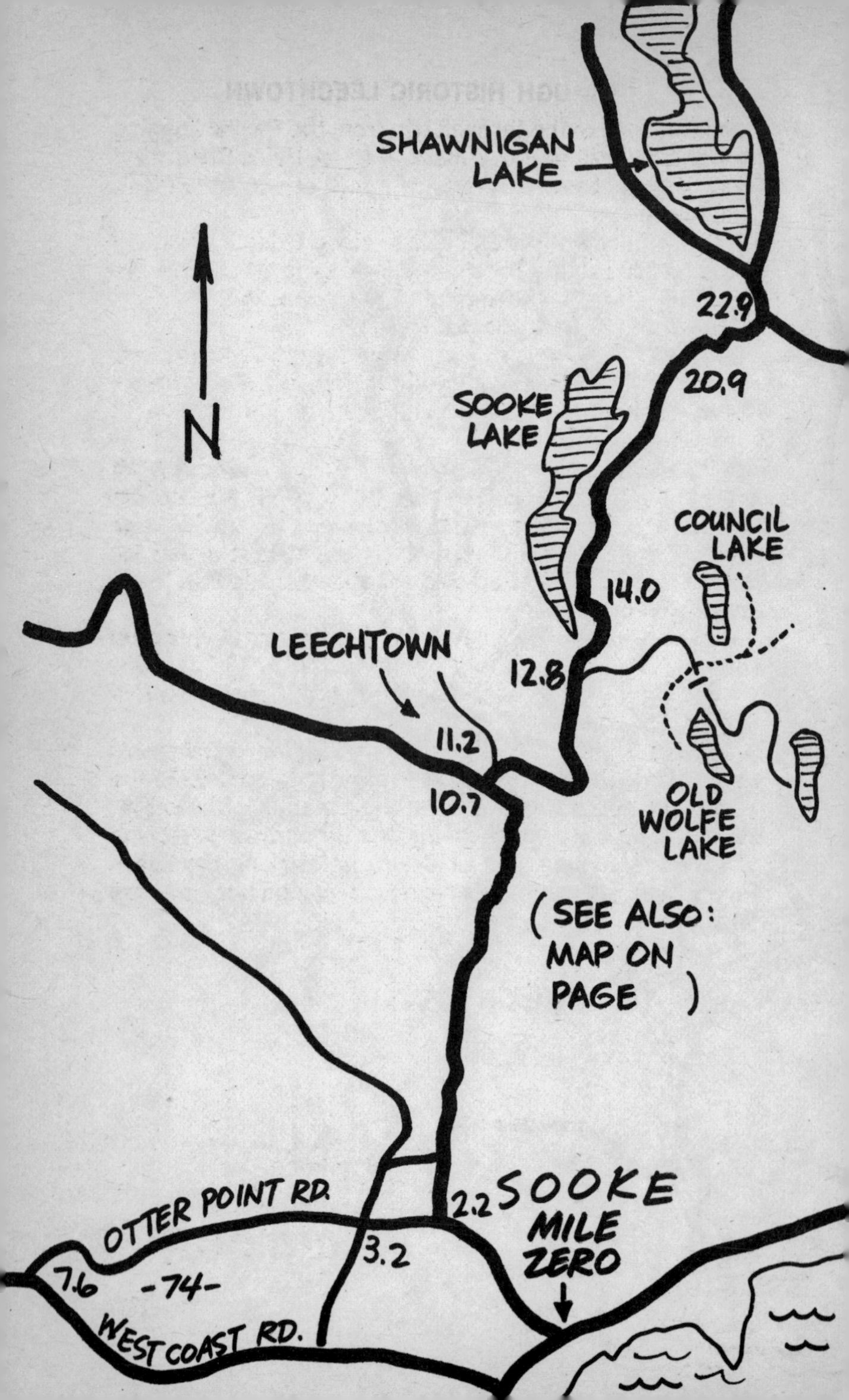

SHAWNIGAN
LAKE ←

22.9

20.9

SOOKE
LAKE

COUNCIL
LAKE

14.0

LEECHTOWN

12.8

11.2

10.7

OLD
WOLFE
LAKE

(SEE ALSO:
MAP ON
PAGE   )

OTTER POINT RD.

2.2   SOOKE
        MILE
3.2   ZERO

7.6   -74-

WEST COAST RD.

THROUGH HISTORIC LEECHTOWN

First let's make the through trip from the Pacific Logging road entrance at mile 2.2 mark of Otter Point Road from Sooke Village, through Leechtown and out to Shawnigan Lake cutoff.

It is 3.2 miles from Sooke village along Otter Point Road to the Butler logging road and 7.6 miles to where you re-enter the West Coast Road at Gordon Beach.

Mile Zero (22.9) — Sooke Village.

Mile 2.2 (20.7) — Turn right along Pacific Logging road.

Drive for 8 1/2 miles, alongside Boneyard Lake, Colledge Creek, Sooke River and Leech River, to intersection at Leech River bridge.

Mile 10.7 (12.2) — Intersection. Straight ahead for 3.5 miles along beautiful Leech River and up very steep hill (we don't advise trying it) to hook up with Weeks Lake Road on right at top of hill, or carry on straight ahead for Butlers Road on left or on straight ahead for Jordan River and Rayonier mainline.

We will describe the Weeks Lake - Butler trips in the next chapter.

Keep right over Leech River bridge for Leechtown and Shawnigan cutoff.

Mile 11.2 (11.7) — Sooke Lake Logging watchman's shack. Left turn for one mile for side trip to beautiful little McDonald Lake. We keep straight ahead for Shawnigan cutoff. This is the area of old historic Leechtown gold camp and there are some nice picnicking holes along the Leech River. Keep left through gate, which sometimes you may find locked.

SOOKE BASIN

To COLWOOD CORNER & VICTORIA

ISLAND HIGHWAY

BUTLERS TO WEEKS LAKE

One of the main access points into the Sooke logging roads network is from Butler log dump at the Mile 18.8 mark of the West Coast Road between Sooke and Jordan River.

We will enter this way for a trip through to Weeks Lake on the Port Renfrew - Bear Creek - Shawnigan Road at the Mile 24 mark.

Mile Zero(27.1) — Butler log dump at the 18.8 mile mark on drive along West Coast Road to Port Renfrew.

The fairly good gravel road winds alongside Kemp Road, but there is no proper access to the lake at this point. You can get to Kemp Lake by the Kemp Lake Road off the West Coast Road before Otter Point. This is a good spring and fall fly fishing lake.

Mile 2.7 (24.24) — Cross Otter Point Road at the 3.2 mile mark from Sooke village. Keep straight ahead on logging road.

Mile 9.1 (18.0) — A road, hardly noticeable on left leads to Tugwell Lake. Only a four-wheel drive vehicle could make it for first 100 yards and then it becomes a fairly good gravel road for half a mile to shores of Tugwell Lake, which has been stocked with fish.

Mile 10.0 (17.1) — Road on left connects with Tugwell mainline.

Mile 10.8 (16.3) — Small pond at side of road. This looks like just a mud hole and is used for a fire station. But we have taken good-sized cutthroat trout from this lake by casting with a Deadly Dick.

Mile 11.8 (15.3) — Road on left leads to Boulder Lake.

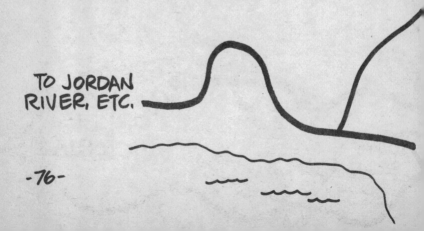

TO JORDAN
RIVER, ETC.

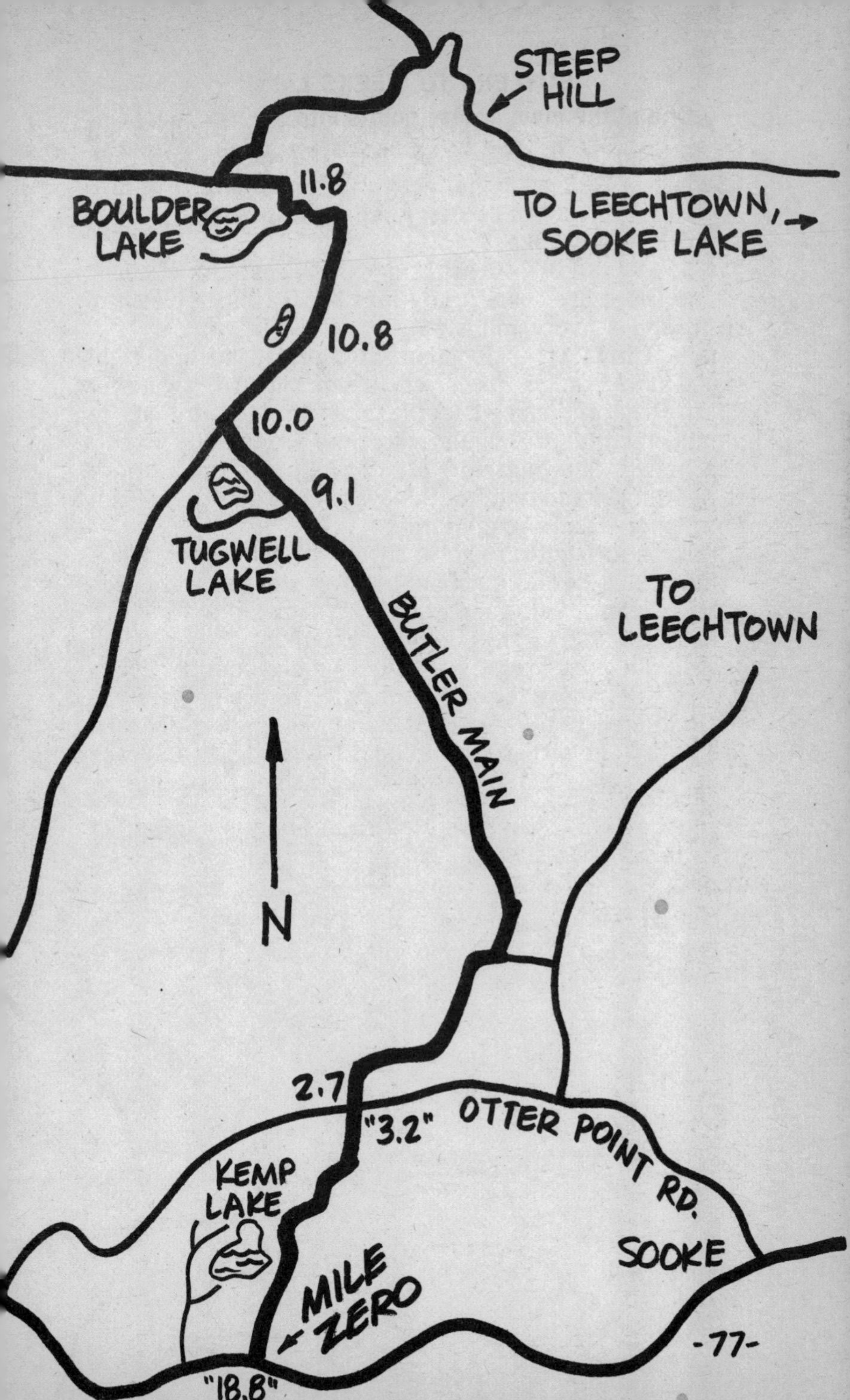

STEEP
HILL

BOULDER
LAKE

11.8

TO LEECHTOWN,
SOOKE LAKE

10.8

10.0

9.1

TUGWELL
LAKE

BUTLER MAIN

TO
LEECHTOWN

N

2.7

"3.2" OTTER POINT RD.

KEMP
LAKE

SOOKE

MILE
ZERO

-77-

"18.8"

Mile 12.0 (15.1) — Quarry and junction. Road to left leads west to Jordan River, B.C. Hydro reservoir and Rayonier's CPS mainline. Active logging along this road could restrict public access. Keep right in easterly direction for Weeks Lake.

Mile 13.1 (14.0) — Cross bridge over west fork of Leech River. There are some pretty falls here, a nice stretch of river, and a panoramic view.

Mile 15 (12.1) — Junction. Straight ahead and right leads for 3.5 miles down very steep hill to bridge over Leech River and along beautiful stretch of Leech River to junction at the 10.7-mile mark of the Otter Point Road - Leechtown - Shawnigan drive. Left over Leech River bridge to Shawnigan and right for Boneyard Lake and Otter Point Road over Pacific Logging road.

But, we turn left at the Mile 15 junction for Weeks Lake.

Mile 19.7 (7.4) — Junction. Right drops down to Leech River canyons. Left goes towards Weeks Lake.

Mile 23.9 (3.2) — After driving through logging slash and grouse shooting areas, you enter timber country above Weeks Lake and after driving through a logging gate you reach intersection where road on left leads short distance to Weeks Lake picnicking and boat launching area. Weeks Lake is a good early season trout fishing lake, but in summer the trout may be wormy.

Mile 25.3 (1.8) — Junction. Left leads to the west side of Weeks Lake and Jordan Meadows. Keep right for Shawnigan - Bear Creek Port Renfrew road. But Jordan Meadows is well worth exploring.

Mile 27.1 (Zero) — Junction with the Bear Creek Road at the Mile 24 mark of that drive.

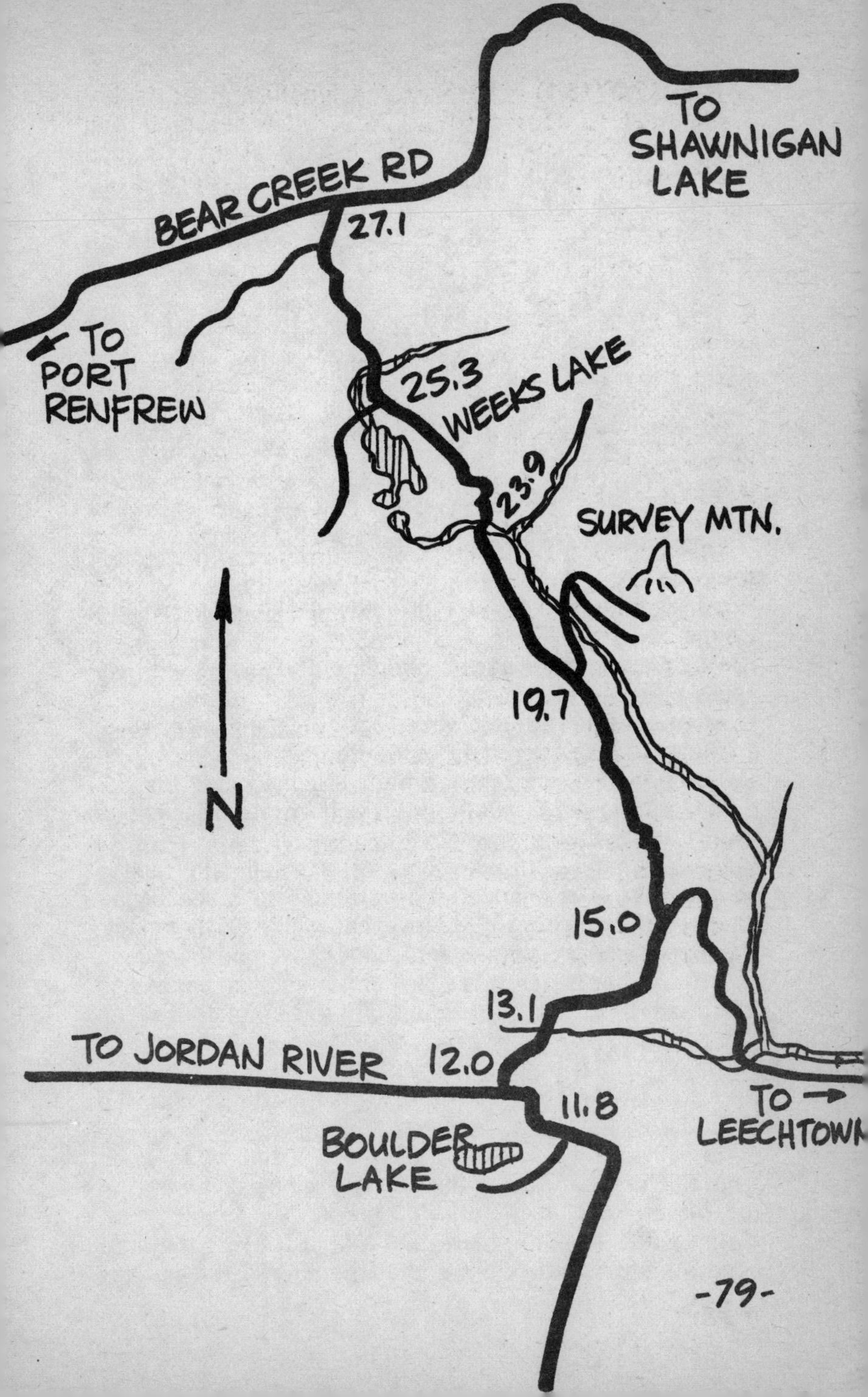

TO
SHAWNIGAN
LAKE

BEAR CREEK RD

27.1

TO
PORT
RENFREW

25.3

WEEKS LAKE

23.9

SURVEY MTN.

N

19.7

15.0

13.1

TO JORDAN RIVER   12.0

11.8

BOULDER
LAKE

TO →
LEECHTOWN

SOOKE LAKES HOLD PROMISE

The Sooke logging area is dotted with little lakes, many of them barren of trout, but holding great potential if they were stocked. Two of them — Ranger and Tugwell — were stocked by the fish and wildlife branch in the late 1960s and as long as public access is assured the provincial authorities would be prepared to stock more of these lakes.

Some are hard to reach and a trail-building program carried out by some organization such as the fish and game clubs, in conjunction with logging companies, might be a good idea. Many anglers would rather hike to a lake than drive to it.

We toured 42 miles of Sooke logging roads with timber operator Ted Shaw, just to have a look at some of these lakes. At the time some of the roads were barred to public travel because of active logging. Other roads were only suitable for four-wheel drive vehicles.

We entered at the Mile 24.4 mark of the West Coast Road, at Anderson Road which led to Old Elder logging claims.

We followed the Tugwell mainline and also used connecting fire access roads.

Six miles in we kept left into an active logging area, which at the time was barred to recreationists.

One mile along on top of a hill we looked east (on our right) for a view of Tugwell Lake, which we later reached off the Butler mainline.

Another mile along we came to a small lake, just a pothole, but it is connected by streams to much bigger Ranger Lake which we found less than a mile further along.

Ranger Lake is Y-shaped and about half a mile long, deep and always has water. It is a real dandy and you can get to it by road. In winter it is a fine skating lake for those who can get to it.

Ranger Lake is the headwater of the east branch of Muir Creek, but downstream falls stop fish getting too far up Muir Creek.

We retraced our way to the Tugwell mainline, followed Tugwell Creek, and two miles further along came out on the Butler Road at the Mile 10 mark.

We turned left and at the 10.8-Mile mark was the little pond we had fished before and at the Mile 11.8 mark was the road on the left, which led 1 1/4 miles to an unnamed lake, which we called Boulder Lake because of huge glacial-deposited boulders jutting out of it. This is a pretty and fairly big lake, muskeg on one side, with an island and then deeper water.

Back on the Butler mainline we went back to the Mile 9.1 mark and turned up that terrible side road leading to Tugwell Lake, which we had originally seen from the high ridge to the west.

There are many other, and bigger lakes in the logging areas, but these were some of the easily accessible lakes.

Some day this Sooke area should be a fisherman's paradise. All that is needed is cooperation between logging companies and the fish and wildlife branch.

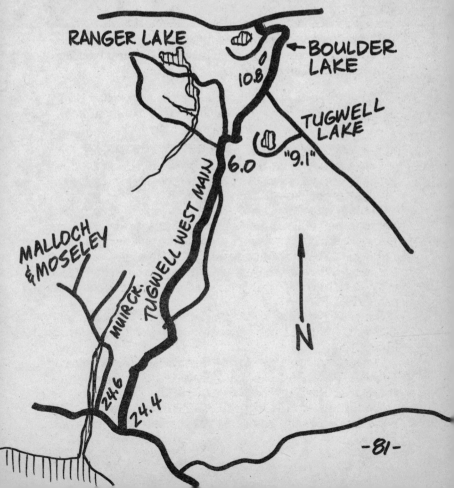

Logging roads lead to beautiful camping areas like this one on shores of Cowichan Lake in B.C. Forest Products Caycuse Campground.

With logging and public roads circling Cowichan Lake anglers look forward to catching trout like these from Shaw Creek area, landed by Al and Mary McPhee.

Logging roads beckon to hunters in the fall and trailbikers Tom Moss and George Goy hit it lucky on Cowichan's 19 Creek slash areas.

LOOP ROADS IN ALL DIRECTIONS
IN MB'S SHAWNIGAN DIVISION

MacMillan Bloedel's Shawnigan Division logging roads connect with several other systems to provide a number of interesting loop trips ... and most of the roads are open on a full-time access basis.

You can even enter this system from Skutz Falls ... over the existing logging bridge, some rather rough connecting road, and end up at Weeks Lake and Sooke or Port Renfrew, at Koksilah's Wild Deer Lake and on to Burnt Bridge, or at Deerholme headquarters of the Division.

Contra-wise you can vary the loops in all directions, with Deerholme as the most likely starting point.

DEERHOLME MAINLINE

Start the trip to Deerholme spots from the Island Highway, just south of the Silver Bridge at Duncan.

Mile Zero (33.8) — Turn west off Island Highway at Koksilah onto old highway into Duncan.

Mile 1.1 (32.7) — White Bridge junction. Bridge on right. Miller Road sharp left. Keep left and centre up Indian Road.

Mile 3.3 (30.5) — After crossing railway track come to junction at Glenora. Keep right.

Mile 3.7 (30.1) — Vaux Road on right leads to Cowichan Fish and Game Club complex and start of Cowichan River Anglers' Footpath. Keep straight ahead for Deerholme.

Mile 4.4 (29.4) — After passing couple of side roads on right you come to MB Shawnigan headquarters, just right before railway tracks. Turn right through yard for logging road.

Mile 4.6 (29.2) — Junction. Keep right. Road on left is another mainline which leads to Lois Lake and Wild Deer Lake. Keep right for this mainline trip.

Mile 5.0 (28.8) — Junction. On right is another entrance on to the mainline we are following.

Mile 5.1 (28.7) — Open gate and start of gravel.

Mile 7.1 (26.7) — Rough road on left should lead to Keating Lake which is being developed as picnicking-fishing site.

Mile 7.2 (26.6) — Another rough road on left.

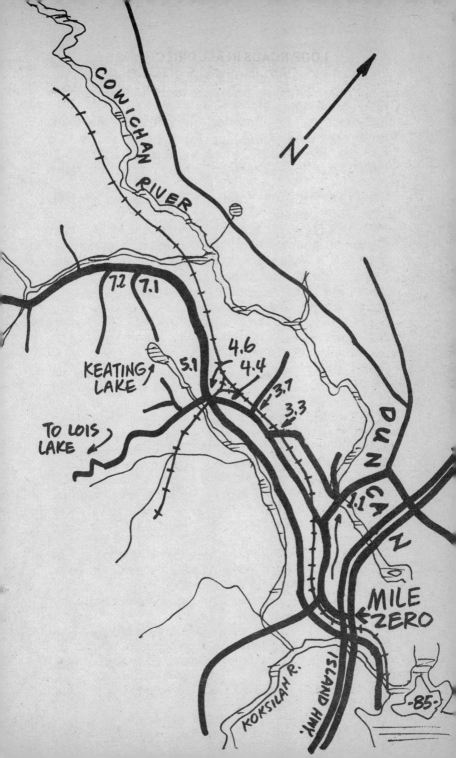

Mile 10.6 (23.2) — After driving up long hill through second growth and mature timber come to junction — up traffic on right. But keep straight ahead for Wild Deer Lake, turning for which comes before the next crossover junction where up and down roads join.

Mile 11.2 (22.6) — Junction. Straight ahead for Skutz Falls, Weeks Lake and M-Line. A left turn leads to Wild Deer Lake and Koksilah, which we describe later.

Mile 12.2 (21.6) — Crossover junction for up and down roads.

Mile 13.8 (20.0) — U-6 Active logging area on right. No access during week.

Mile 15.4 (18.4) — Junction. Straight ahead, and later right, for 7.8 miles to Skutz Falls loop and we describe that trip later. Continuing straight ahead goes to active logging areas at head of Fleet Creek. We turn left for Kapoor - Weeks Lake Loop.

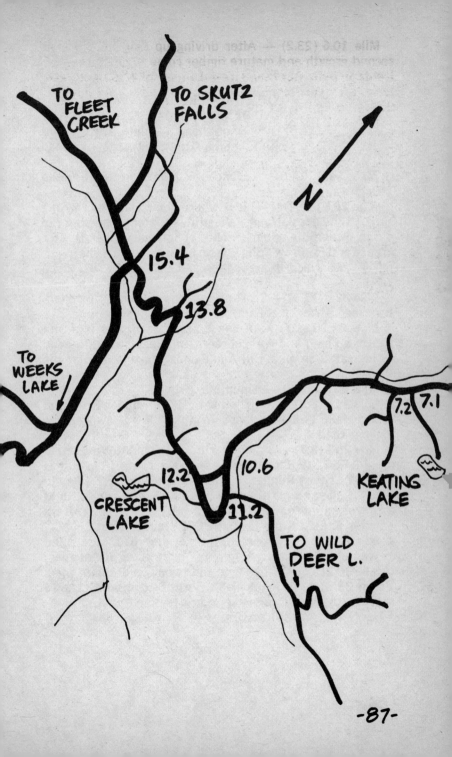

TO FLEET CREEK

TO SKUTZ FALLS

N

15.4

13.8

TO WEEKS LAKE

7.2 7.1

12.2

10.6

KEATING LAKE

CRESCENT LAKE

11.2

TO WILD DEER L.

LOOP TO WEEKS LAKE
AND RENFREW ROAD

Mile 17.3 (16.5) — Keep on the M mainline. At this point there is junction with F line on right. Keep straight ahead on M.

Mile 19.8 (14.0) — Junction. X-line on right. Keep straight ahead on M.

Mile 20.6 (13.2) — This is where you could make wrong turn. M-line goes straight ahead to an interesting stand of old trees and the upper reaches of San Juan River. But for Weeks and Renfrew - Shawnigan Lake loops turn sharp left on K-Line, which is a rougher and apparently less used road.

Mile 22.0 (11.8) — Cross stream and K Road turn on left. But keep straight ahead.

Mile 22.1 (11.7) — A-line crosses road, but it is not shown on map and we ignored it and keep straight ahead as indicated on map. But A-line does join this road at the 22.8 mark.

Mile 23.2 (10.6) — Open MB gate.

Mile 25.0 (8.8) — Junction with BCFP Kapoor Road and A-line main. Left turn leads to Koksilah - Shawnigan by logging road.

Mile 25.1 (8.7) — Junction with government gravel road (mile 24 on the Bear Creek - Shawnigan trip from Harris Creek Y at Port Renfrew). Straight ahead for 3.2 miles to Weeks Lake and on to Sooke logging road network. Right on government road for Harris Creek Y and Port Renfrew. Left for Koksilah, paralleling BCFP Kapoor Road.

Mile 27.2 (6.6) — Junction with logging road. Turn right, as we do, or you can carry on up hill on government road.

Mile 30.2 (3.6) — Open gate and rejoin government road.

Mile 33.8 (zero) — Koksilah's Burnt Bridge, which is also reached by Wild Deer Lake loop described next.

Carry on from Burnt Bridge to Shawnigan Lake.

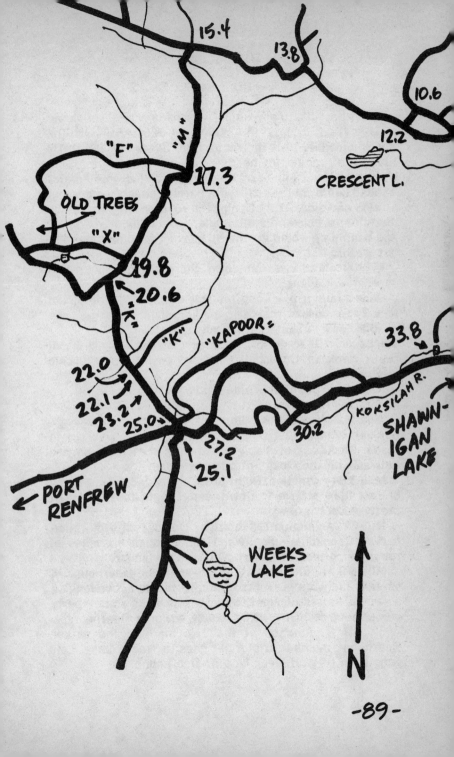

15.4

13.8

10.6

"M"

"F"

12.2

CRESCENT L.

17.3

OLD TREES

"X"

19.8

20.6

"K"

"K"

"KAPOOR"

33.8

22.0

22.1

23.2

25.0

27.2

30.2

KOKSILAH R.

SHAWN-
IGAN
LAKE

25.1

PORT
RENFREW

WEEKS
LAKE

N

LOOP FROM SKUTZ FALLS

It is possible to enter the Deerholme area through old logging roads across the bridge at Skutz Falls on the Cowichan River. But the roads from Skutz can be pretty rough and at one point, heading up a narrow mountain trail we came across a huge rock — about five feet in diameter — dead center of the road, with barely enough room to get around one side. At that point the road became not much more than a hole and a ditch filled with slimy mud and we had doubts we would get the Balboa motor home around it, but we did.

At that point, in a rainstorm, there can be no turning back in any event.

Here is our trip, joining the Deerholme mainline at the Mile 14.5 mark of the early mainline trip.

Mile Zero — Skutz Falls bridge.

Mile .6 — Road on left leads downstream to vicinity of south bank of Cowichan River, opposite Stoltz picnic ground.

There are a number of side roads, mostly unused, but we keep straight ahead.

Mile 2.8 — After winding hill we come to the huge boulder, which must be close to start of MB Deerholme roads. Rock was probably originally placed as a barrier between the two logging road networks.

Mile 3.8 — Junction. Right probably leads to some caves on secondary MB road, but we keep straight ahead through pretty second growth.

Mile 6 — A junction T. Keep right. On our first exploration trip we turned left and wandered through six miles of roads which seemed to go nowhere in particular.

Mile 6.8 — Junction with MB S-line from Deerholme, a smooth and wide gravel road. Right goes to active logging and headwaters of Fleet River, which holds some sporty pan-sized trout. But, we keep left, towards Deerholme.

Mile 7.8 — Junction at the 15.4 mark of the earlier Deerholme mainline trip. Right goes to Weeks Lake. Left goes back to Wild Deer loop or Deerholme.

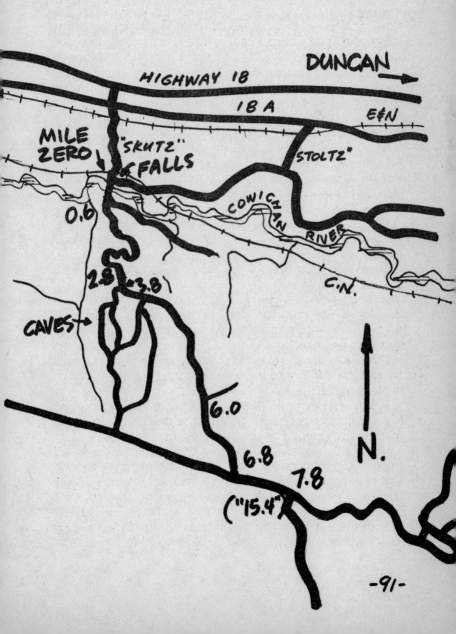

DUNCAN →

HIGHWAY 18

18 A

E&N

MILE ZERO

"SKUTZ" FALLS

"STOLTZ"

0.6

COWICHAN RIVER

2.8   ("3.8")

C.N.

CAVES →

6.0

N.

6.8

7.8

("15.4")

LOOP TO WILD DEER, KOKSILAH

Mile 11.2 — This is the junction on the Deerholme Mainline trip where you keep left for Wild Deer Lake and Koksilah.

Mile 11.7 — Rough road on left. Keep straight ahead ignoring spur roads.

Mile 12.1 — Major junction. Up hill on left should go to Lois Lake and back to Deerholme, but we didn't make that trip. Keep ahead and right.

Mile 14.1 — Junction. Sharp right for one-tenth mile to Wild Deer Lake. This road gets washed out in winter. Middle Road on right goes to Silver Mine Trail and eventually to Crescent Lake and back on to M-line for Weeks Lake, but that is another exploration. Wild Deer Lake is an excellent trout fishing lake and there is a road to the lake for launching small boats and there is some camping space for vehicles. Keep straight ahead for Koksilah.

Mile 16.2 — Drive along narrow road with cliff on left and fair amount of fallen rock on road.

Mile 16.7 — "No hunting" signs and indications of small development on right.

Mile 18.2 — After following logging roads, not much more than new trails, you reach junction and first class logging road. Right leads to logging gate and active logging. Keep left for Koksilah. The MB maps don't show this road connecting with the Burnt Bridge, but it does.

Mile 20.7 — Burnt Bridge over Koksilah. This new logging road has been built above the old trails we once knew to the Koksilah River. Half a mile back along the logging road a side road leads to the Koksilah riverside primitive camping and picnicking areas.

From the Burnt Bridge it is 3.1 miles to the West Arm Road around Shawnigan Lake, 6.1 miles to the junction at Mason's Store and Patio at the head of the lake, 6.4 miles to Shawnigan Village, and 9.8 miles to the Island Highway at Mill Bay.

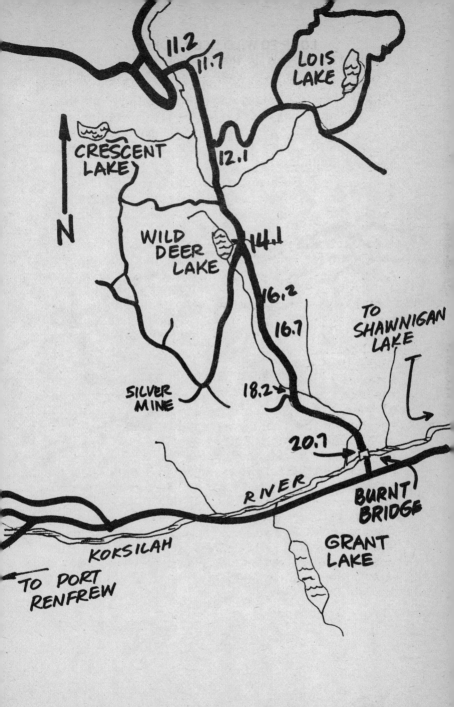

11.2
11.7

LOIS
LAKE

CRESCENT
LAKE

N

12.1

WILD
DEER
LAKE

14.1

16.2

16.7

TO
SHAWNIGAN
LAKE

SILVER
MINE

18.2

20.7

RIVER

BURNT
BRIDGE

KOKSILAH

GRANT
LAKE

TO PORT
RENFREW

COWICHAN LAKE CIRCLE TRIP

Colonist King Fisherman entries show Cowichan Lake as the undisputed year-round producer of big cutthroat and rainbow trout, along with some hefty Dolly Varden.

A 47.9-mile long road circles the lake, half of it government road and the other half all-hours-public-access logging roads. Along the way are cabin resorts, private tenting grounds...

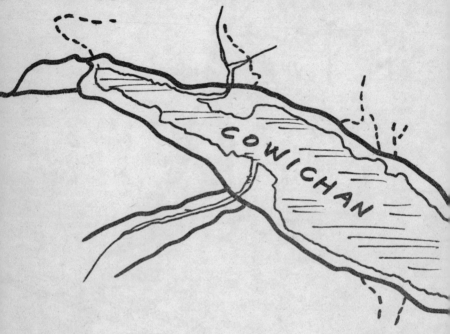

LAKE COWICHAN
AREA

provincial parks, forest service stopovers and forest company campgrounds, to say nothing of a number of places to launch boats for fishing.

The forests back of Cowichan Lake are favorite grouse and deer hunting areas and the Shaw Creek regions are the home of one band of Vancouver Island Roosevelt elk.

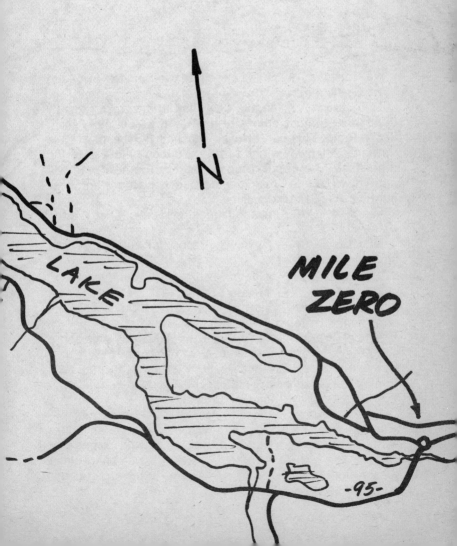

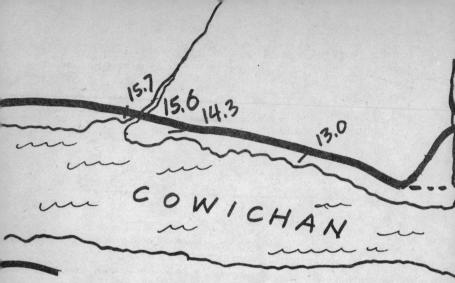

We start our Cowichan Lake circle trip from the bridge at Lake Cowichan.

Mile Zero (47.9) — Lake Cowichan bridge, turn right by Riverside Inn, just before bridge for the Youbou - North Shore Road. This can also be reached by the new Lake Cowichan Highway which turns to Youbou before entering the village. The upper Youbou Road or the new road will take you to Meade Creek logging roads for grouse and deer hunting, huckleberry picking.

Mile .8 (47.1) — Kinsmen launching ramp, just above the weir.

Mile 1.6 (46.3) — Castaway Resort for cottages, tents, fishing, water skiing.

Mile 2.9 (45.0) — Cedar Resort, boat launching.

Mile 3.6 (44.3) — Meade Creek.

Mile 4.3 (43.6) — View of north arm of Cowichan Lake and then turn left to rejoin Youbou Road.

Mile 9.0 (39.8) — After skirting lake and lakeshore homes you come to lumbering town of Youbou. A left turn will take you to Saseenos area, marina, launching and tenting. Gas stations in Youbou, and a good idea to fill up if you are heading Nitinat - Bamfield way.

Mile 10.1 (37.8) — B. C. Forest Products headquarters and mill where you start gravel portion of North Shore industrial road and limited access. A sign welcomes you and sets out rules of entrance. Three tenths of a mile along road swings sharp right for big hairpin turn which cuts out old Cottonweed Creek bridge.

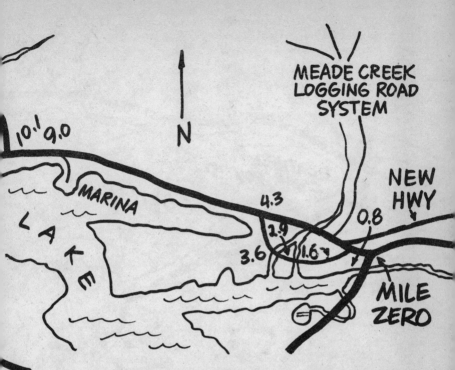

The B. C. forest service has a new and expanding program to provide small camping and picnic sites in many timber areas favored by public travellers. Plan is to select desireable recreation stopping places and to provide access, parking, sanitation facilities and litter barrels, with a minimum amount of disturbance to the natural beauties of the areas. In fact, these places in some instances, will have so little disturbance the public may have difficulty finding them. They will be designed for the recreationists who seek to get away from the crowds.

Two of these sites are along this North Shore Road .... at Pine Point, west of Youbou and near the proposed Cottonwood provincial campground, and at Maple Grove in the Wardroper Creek area.

Mile 13.0 (34.9) — Pine Point BCFS campground.

Mile 14.3 (33.6) — Maple Grove BCFS campground.

Mile 15.6 (32.3) — Wardroper Creek. The mouth of this creek is one of the Cowichan Lake fishing hot spots.

Mile 15.7 (32.2) — Logging gate, open when access permitted. Signs warn about deer and elk crossing.

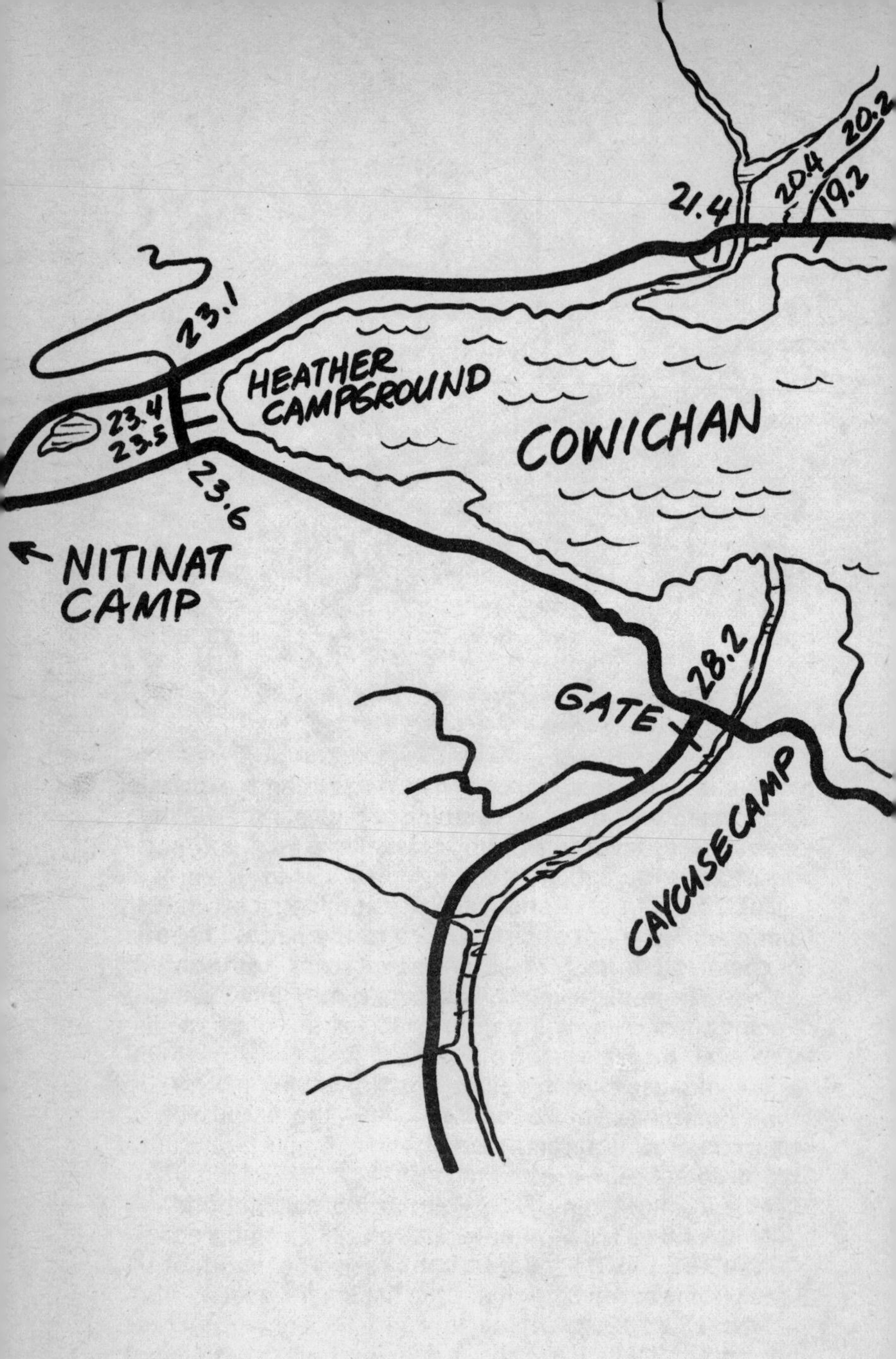

2

23.1

HEATHER
CAMPGROUND

COWICHAN

23.4
23.5

23.6

← NITINAT
CAMP

21.4   20.4   20.2
        19.2

28.2

GATE

CAYCUSE CAMP

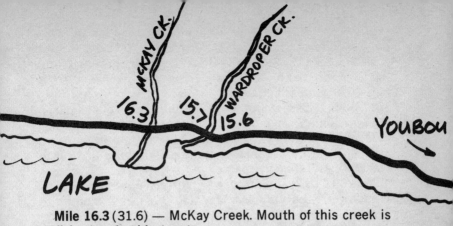

Mile 16.3 (31.6) — McKay Creek. Mouth of this creek is well known for big trout.

Mile 19.2 (28.7) — Road on left leads to three car primitive camping area.

Mile 20.2 (27.7) — Little Shaw main on right.

Mile 20.4 (27.5) — Little Shaw Creek, and this creek, which looks exceptionally inviting to fishermen, skirts the road for a short distance. Mouth of Shaw Creek is another hot fishing spot for big trout.

Mile 21.4 (26.5) — Shaw Creek. Roads on left lead to primitive camping areas near creek mouth.

Mile 23.1 (24.8) — Junction. Left for campground and picnic site and south shore road. Straight ahead one mile for Nitinat Camp of Crown Zellerbach. Logging road goes up hill on right. We turn left for lake circle tour and on to Nitinat country.

Mile 23.4 (24.5) — Left for B.C. Forest Products Heather Campground, a delightful spot among trees on the lakeshore. Good base for fishing, swimming and hunting.

Mile 23.5 (24.4) — Left for beach, for boat launching and overflow camping.

Mile 23.6 (24.3) — Junction. Right turn goes to Nitinat Lake - Bamfield areas. Left turn to Caycuse and South Shore Road back along Cowichan Lake, and we continue on our circle trip around the lake.

Mile 28.2 (19.7) — Junction with Caycuse logging road. Right goes into logging operations for hunting and Caycuse River steelhead areas and for alternative skyline route to Nitinat area, providing opportunity for Nitinat loop trip for Sunday or weekend driving. That trip will be covered in Nitinat road system chapters.

Mile 28.9 (19.0) — Caycuse industrial camp. Gas stations, coffee shop and groceries.

Mile 32.5 (15.4) — BCFP Caycuse campground and picnic site, shelter, boat launching and excellent trout fishing around islands.

Mile 35.4 (12.5) — Bottom of big hill. Chains are required in snow conditions and even with them this is a tough hill.

Mile 36.5 (11.4) — Top of big hill.

Mile 39.0 (8.9) — Leave gravel logging road and on to blacktop government road.

Mile 39.2 (8.7) — Entrance to Western Forest Industries Wildflower Reserve. April, May and June best months to visit.

Mile 39.9 (8.0) — Honeymoon Bay. Junction with Walton Road. Turn extreme left on to Walton for short distance to Gordon Bay provincial campground and boat launching. A big and popular campground. Boat and canoe rentals are available close to campground.

Mile 40.1 (7.8) — Sutton Creek and big private tenting, boat launching and fishing resort.

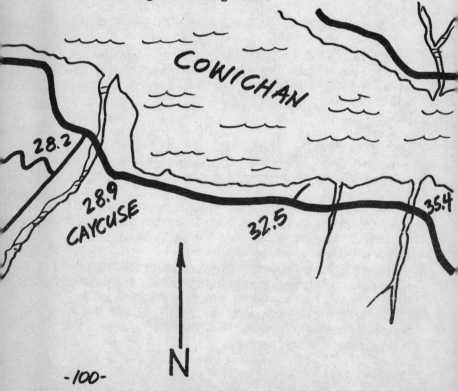

Mile 40.4 (7.5) — Gordon River Road on right is an industrial logging road.

Western Forest Industries has more than 93 miles of road and 20,000 acres of timberland in its Gordon River operations, reached from this industrial road. Ninety per cent of these roads are open to public access during weekend and holiday non-operational hours. They reach Gordon River steelheading pools and deer and grouse hunting areas.

The first 7 1/2 miles of the access road from Honeymoon Bay are open to recreationists at all times, but logging trucks use the road, so be careful.

For a great many miles the roads parallel the 26-mile-long Gordon River and the Loop River and the claims border the BCFP Caycuse operations.

Mile 40.8 (7.1) — Ashburnham Creek.

Mile 42.2 (5.5) — Entrance to Ashburnham Beach, a picnic area with boat launching facilities, made available by Western Forest Industries.

Mile 42.8 (5.1) — Robertson Creek.

Mile 43.6 (4.3) — Mesachie Lake community. A right turn goes to McKenzie Logging and start of road to Port Renfrew - San Juan country.

Mile 46.6 (1.3) — Kiwanis Club Lakeview Park.

Mile 47.9 (Zero) — Bridge in Lake Cowichan and end of circle tour around Cowichan Lake.

SKYLINE ROAD TO NITINAT

Logging road travel can be enhanced by loop roads and an interesting Sunday or weekend loop road drive is to the Nitinat area through the Caycuse skyline roads, into Nitinat River country and back the usual Nitinat Road via Cowichan Lake way, which will be described in another chapter.

It is 26 miles by the BCFP Caycuse - Jasper route to the Nitinat bridge junction, compared to 17 miles the usual way, which starts with the Crown Zellerbach mainline from the junction at the head of Cowichan Lake, on to BCFP roads and on to MacMillan Bloedel Roads.

The old way is easiest, but the new Caycuse way is more adventuresome.

Signs at both ends of the BCFP roads warn of steep hills and that recreationists shouldn't attempt to tow trailers over the route.

The road at the Caycuse gate (Mile 28.2 on the Cowichan Lake Circle Trip) is open during non-operating hours for recreation travel and it starts with a steep hill. By the time you reach the headwaters of the Caycuse River you will have climbed 1,550 feet.

To get over the Jasper Creek divide and down into the Nitinat you climb 2,100 feet and then to get down to the Nitinat road you drop pretty well all of that distance in three steeply winding, and in winter, muddy and slippery miles.

The Jasper and Caycuse lines were first linked for public use in the summer of 1970.

Caycuse River is a good steelhead-producing stream in August, September and late winter months, but to fish it requires some canyon-crawling, down long and slippery banks.

One favorite hole is reached along the McClure mainline (which goes six miles to a dead end) to the end of C49 spur until you see a well-marked trail to upper Caycuse pools.

There are a couple of places to get to fishing holes off the Caycuse mainline in the 10-Mile Creek area. Along the mainline towards the Jasper mainline, entry to the well-fished Meat Hole is near the junction of C9 and C1 spurs.

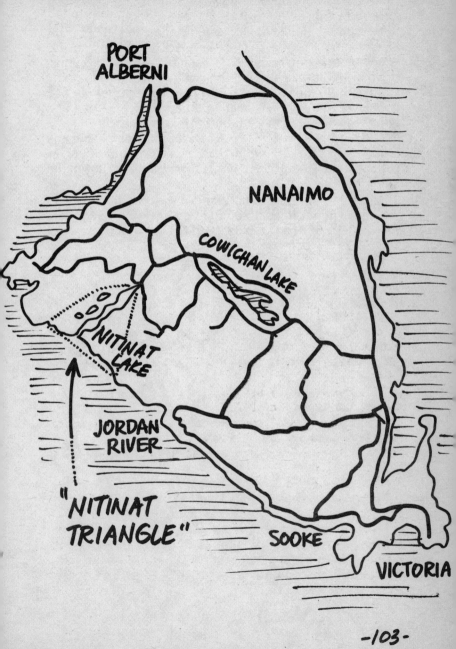

PORT ALBERNI

NANAIMO

COWICHAN LAKE

NITINAT LAKE

JORDAN RIVER

"NITINAT TRIANGLE"

SOOKE

VICTORIA

Let's take the Caycuse trip to Nitinat:

Mile Zero — Caycuse gate (mile 28.2 on Cowichan Lake Circle Trip), now open in non-operational hours. A steep hill starts trip.

Mile 6.9 — Junction. McClure mainline on left. Straight ahead on right for Caycuse-Jasper. McClure River has falls which block fish passage upstream and although you can drive to McClure Lake it only holds tiddler fish.

Mile 17.7 — Junction, and sign pointing right for Nitinat.

Mile 17.8 — Another junction. Keep straight ahead and left. Steep hill on right leads only to logging area.

Mile 19.5 — Junction. Left for Caycuse mainline, but the road doesn't yet link with road along Caycuse River at Nitinat Lake. Keep right on Jasper mainline, down the steep hill.

Mile 22.8 — Bottom of hill and join the road that leads to mainline Nitinat Road. Keep right on one-way road to join up with Nitinat Road at Mile 7.8 of Nitinat trip, or enter at the 10.9 Mile point.

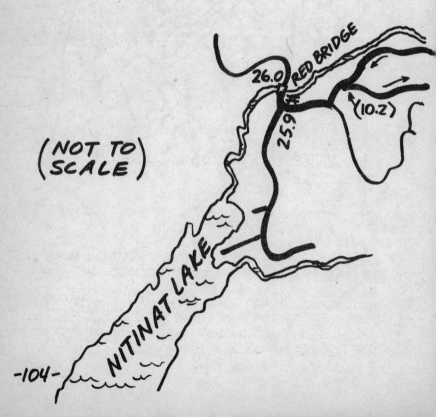

(NOT TO SCALE)

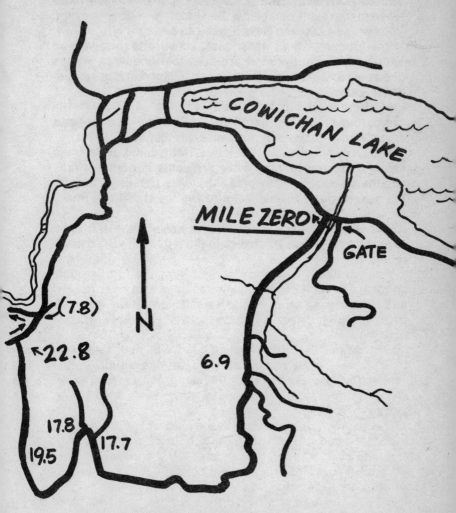

COWICHAN LAKE

MILE ZERO

GATE

N

(7.8)

22.8

6.9

17.8

17.7

19.5

Mile 25.9 — MB-forest service picnic site on banks of Nitinat River, just above bridge. This is one place to start a drift — by boat or canoe, of the Nitinat River.

Mile 26 — Junction at red bridge. Left goes to Nitinat Lake. Right to Bamfield - Port Alberni. Both will be described in other Nitinat chapters. Red bridge becomes Mile Zero for other trips.

RIVER CAMPGROUND AND TUCK LAKE

In May of 1973 Crown Zellerbach opened a wilderness-type campground alongside the Upper Nitinat River on a 24-hour-a-day, seven-days-a-week basis.

The upper Nitinat falls, just above the bridge and abutting the campground are fairy-tale beautiful, with a deep pool and slow reach above and a long reach of smooth water below.

In summer the upper pools with the sandbar at the campground make excellent swimming water and downstream is used by kayakers and canoers.

The Upper Nitinat holds native trout, but a mile or so below these upper falls, there are some impassable falls and the steelhead, cutthroats and Dollys, that come in from the sea, through Nitinat Lake to the lower Nitinat River, don't get to the upper regions.

Sometimes there is good fishing around the CZ campground and further upstream to the falls at the Branch 20 road.

You can follow along on the right from the campground on the CZ Branch 2 road to all-times upstream river fishing and to swimming spots. You can also follow up the main CZ Nitinat road, but that is only open during non-operational hours.

The main CZ Nitinat logging road will now take you through to the Nanaimo Lakes operations although the connecting road can be rough travelling, especially in snow or wet weather, as at the time of writing it was in an active logging area.

The mainline road, reached at the gate which is 4.4 miles from the head of Cowichan Lake (Mile Zero for this trip and mile 23.6 for the Cowichan Lake circle trip) follows the Nitinat River for miles, with plenty of spur roads off to the left to give access to the river.

In 1973 the road was paved for 9.8 miles, at which time you were getting into fairly high territory.

As soon as leaving the pavement at the 9.8 mile mark, Branch 35 access road is on the right and it winds up the mountain through canyons and switchbacks, over the summit to the Nanaimo Lakes operations.

Tuck Lake, which is really two roads separated by a grassy marsh through which you can row a boat, is rated as

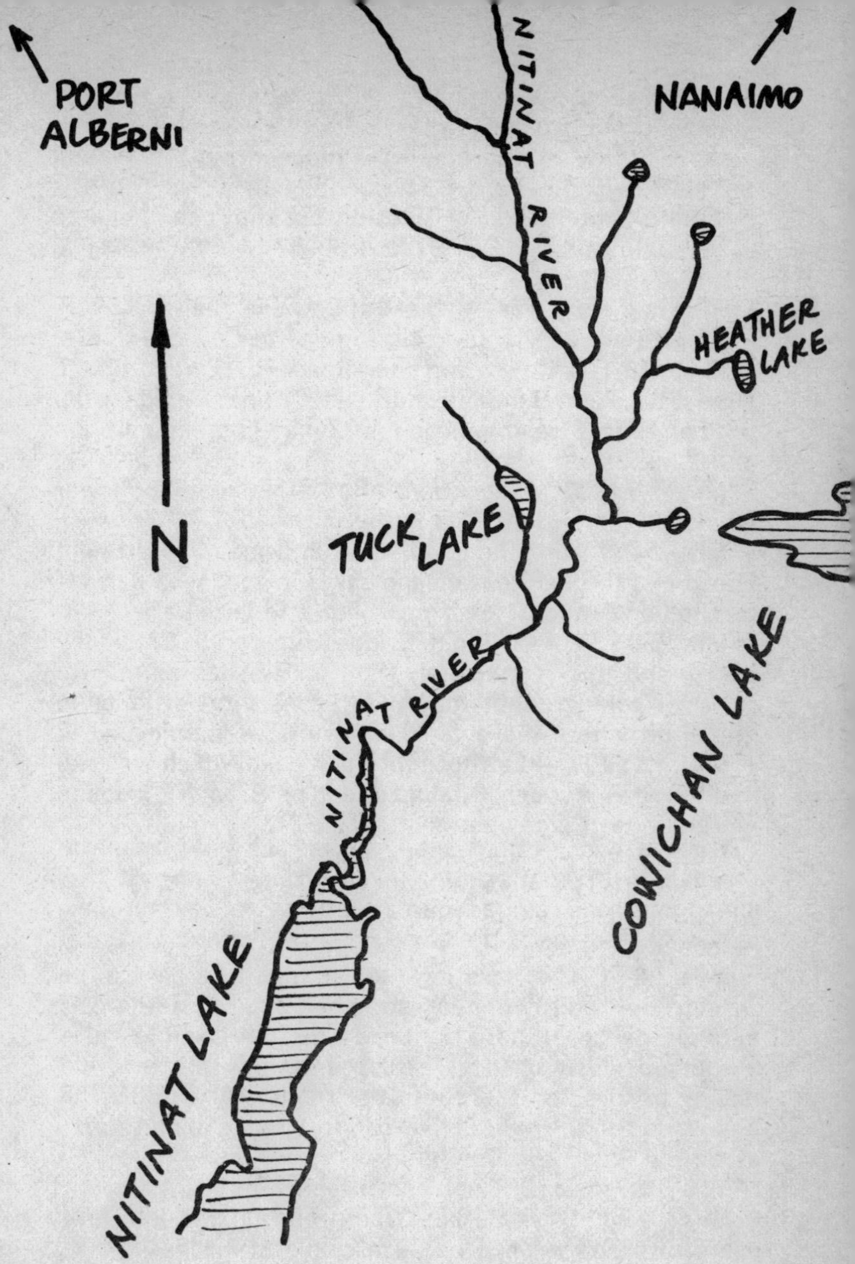

PORT
ALBERNI

NANAIMO

NITINAT RIVER

HEATHER
LAKE

N

TUCK LAKE

NITINAT RIVER

COWICHAN LAKE

NITINAT LAKE

a pretty good trout lake and it is reported sometimes steelhead that run up Parker Creek are taken in the lake.

From the CZ campground it is reached by 7.2 miles of both CZ and B.C. Forest Service logging trails. There is primitive camping area at lakeside, but the road in can be very rough, although BCFP crews do grade it in the spring.

Here is the trip from the head of Cowichan Lake.

Mile Zero (12.2) — Junction at head of Cowichan Lake.

Mile 1.8 (10.4) — Junction. Road to Lower Nitinat, Nitinat Lake and Bamfield on the left, Nitinat logging camp road on right. Straight ahead for CZ mainline, campground and Tuck Lake.

Mile 3.5 (8.7) — Junction. Alternative road for lower Nitinat areas on left. This is the old road.

Mile 4.4 (7.8) — Junction. Gate and mainline straight ahead and through to Nanaimo Lakes in good weather. We turn left on Branch 2 for campground and Tuck Lake.

Mile 5.0 (7.2) — Nitinat Bridge Number 5. Cross the bridge and turn immediately right for two-tenths mile to riverside campground. Road on left goes short distance to gravel pit where there could be overflow camping.

Mile 5.1 (7.1) — Left turn for Tuck Lake, which we take and the road is rough. Straight ahead on Branch 2 leads to more Nitinat River upstream spots.

Mile 5.9 (6.3) — Keep left again for Tuck Lake.

Mile 6.1 (6.1) — Sign tells you you are now in BCFP area which was clearcut in 1940-45 and has been naturally reseeded.

Mile 7.8 (4.4) — Here is where it would be easy to go wrong. The road continues straight ahead, but there is another road, real sharp right like a hairpin. Dead ahead is a spot obviously used as a turn around circle to avoid having to turn too sharply to the road on the right. The upper road on the right is the road to Tuck Lake and starts as an old logging railway grade.

Mile 10.4 (1.8) — Tumbledown shack on right.

Mile 10.7 (1.5) — Parker Creek road on the left, now overgrown and unused because of blown bridges.

Mile 11.9 (0.3) — First glimpse of Tuck Lake.

Mile 12.2 (zero) — Tuck Lake boat launching and wilderness camping area on left.

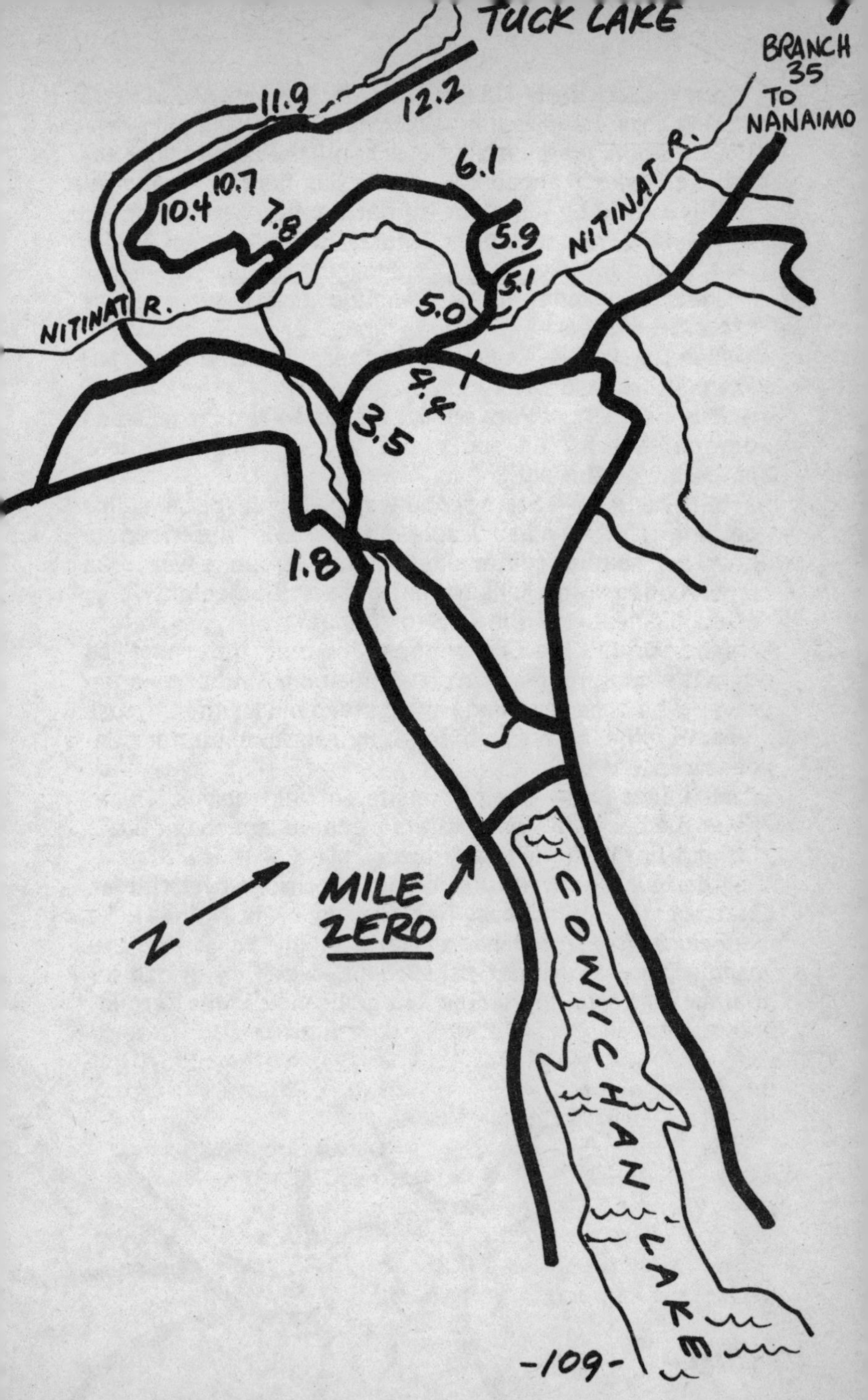

TUCK LAKE

BRANCH
35
TO
NANAIMO

11.9   12.2

6.1

10.4 10.7   5.9
        7.8
              5.1
NITINAT R.
        5.0
NITINAT R.

        4.4

      3.5

1.8

N →

MILE
ZERO ↑

COWICHAN LAKE

ENTER NITINAT FROM COWICHAN LAKE

Mile Zero(11.9) — Junction at Head of Cowichan Lake — the 23.6-mile mark on the Cowichan Lake circle trip. Keep right, or straight ahead for Nitinat - Bamfield - Port Alberni.

Mile 1.8(10.1) — Left for Nitinat country. Straight ahead would take you to Upper Nitinat River 24-hour access campground, Tuck Lake and CZ logging roads which follow Nitinat River and on to Nanaimo Lakes system. See separate chapter.

Mile 5.6 (6.3) — Leave BCFP operations and enter MB Franklin River division.

Mile 6.0 (5.9) — Path on right leads to Nitinat falls and downstream fishing spots, but you may have to look carefully for the path.

Mile 7.8 (4.1) — Start of one-way traffic, Jasper mainline on left. The Caycuse-Jasper-Nitinat loop described in previous chapter, enters midway on this one-way road (coming back) and joins Nitinat Road at this point. We go straight ahead for one-way to Nitinat.

Mile 10.9 (1.0) — End of one-way traffic. Returning you take the upper one-way road at this point and carry on in reverse, or turn right midway up steep hill for the Caycuse loop, which can be rough and only recommended for adventure.

Mile 11.8 (.1) — MB picnic site on right beside Nitinat River ... a beautiful spot and the place we launch our boats to float down the Nitinat River.

Mile 11.9 (Zero) — Junction at Red Bridge over Nitinat. Left goes 5.9 miles, past Red Rock pool, to Nitinat Lake launching (see next chapter) and to MB-Forest Service campground on Nitinat Lake. Right, over Red Bridge for Bamfield - Port Alberni. Red Bridge becomes Mile Zero for other trips.

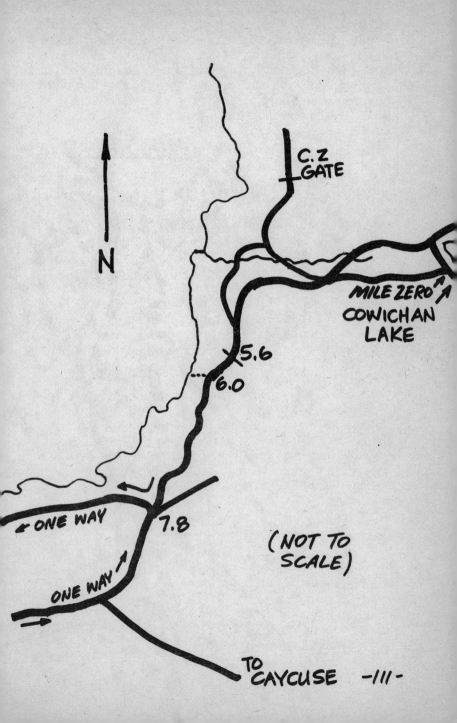

C.Z GATE

MILE ZERO
COWICHAN
LAKE

X 5.6
6.0

ONE WAY

7.8

(NOT TO SCALE)

ONE WAY

TO CAYCUSE   -111-

FOLLOW RIVER TO CAMPGROUND
Mile Zero — Nitinat red bridge intersection. Keep left.
Mile 2.4 — Red Rock Pool. The most popular fishing place on the Nitinat River, and one spot where you may pull out after a short boat drift from just above the bridge at the picnic ground. If you don't pull out here you are in for quite a long drift and a possible stretch of rough water at head of lake to reach lakeshore pullout spots.

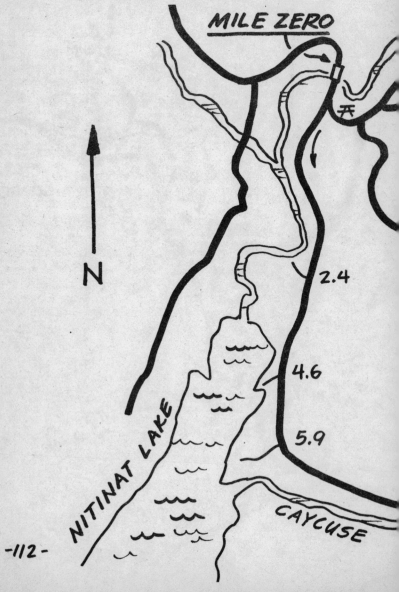

Mile 4.6— Right turn leads to wharf and launching ramp at head of Nitinat Lake.

Mile 5.3— Right turn leads to new Indian village, most of which was transferred from Clo-oose on the west coast trail.

Mile 5.9 — Right for three-quarter mile to MB - forest service campground on Nitinat Lake.

The campground includes boat launching ramp and is in delightful treed area along log-strewn Nitinat Lake. Remember there are dangerous daytime winds on Nitinat Lake. Boating must be done in early mornings or evenings. Only boating experts should fish around or try crossing dangerous Nitinat Bar at foot of lake, and then only after obtaining expert local advice as to proper tides and the hazards.

From the turning into the campground you can drive straight ahead for short distance and you can walk down to mouth of Caycuse River.

It is this road that may some day connect up with the Caycuse mainline, mentioned in the Caycuse - Nitinat chapter.

BLIND
ROAD

RIVER

CANOE NITINAT TRIANGLE LAKES

The Nitinat Triangle, which includes Hobiton, Squalicum and Tsusiat Lakes is destined to become one of the glamor wilderness recreation areas of Vancouver Island.

It is the spot where canoers are able to make an idyllic trip around the circle and if they wish they may hike or portage down the Tsusiat River to beautiful Tsusiat Falls on the West Coast Trail.

It is likely the Nitinat Triangle Lakes will be included in Pacific Rim National Park, but whether or not they are, it is certain their natural beauty and solitude will be preserved for recreation.

The logging roads reach some distance along the west shore of Nitinat Lake to Knob Point picnic site and launching spot, which provides a base for Nitinat Triangle campers and canoers.

We will take the trip from the Nitinat Red Bridge to the Knob Point site, and to the existing end of the road.

Mile Zero — Nitinat red bridge.

Mile 1.5 — Junction. Left for Hobiton and Knob Point. Straight ahead for Flora Lake, Bamfield and Port Alberni, which will be described in other chapters. We keep left.

Mile 2 — Little Nitinat River bridge. Upstream is a beautiful deep pool, an area which should be preserved as a pocket park. Downstream is some riverbank logging, which should never have been allowed under a multiple use plan.

Mile 7.5 — Hobiton dock and boat launching spot and Knob Hill picnic site.

Mile 10 — End of road, at least at time of publishing. If integrated use concept is carried through road will continue few miles to Hobiton lake, where all recreationists could enjoy trip around the three lakes, and probably a short access trail to explore part of Pacific Rim Park West Coast Life Saving Trail.

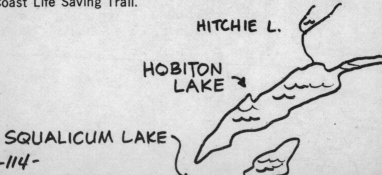

HITCHIE L.

HOBITON LAKE

SQUALICUM LAKE

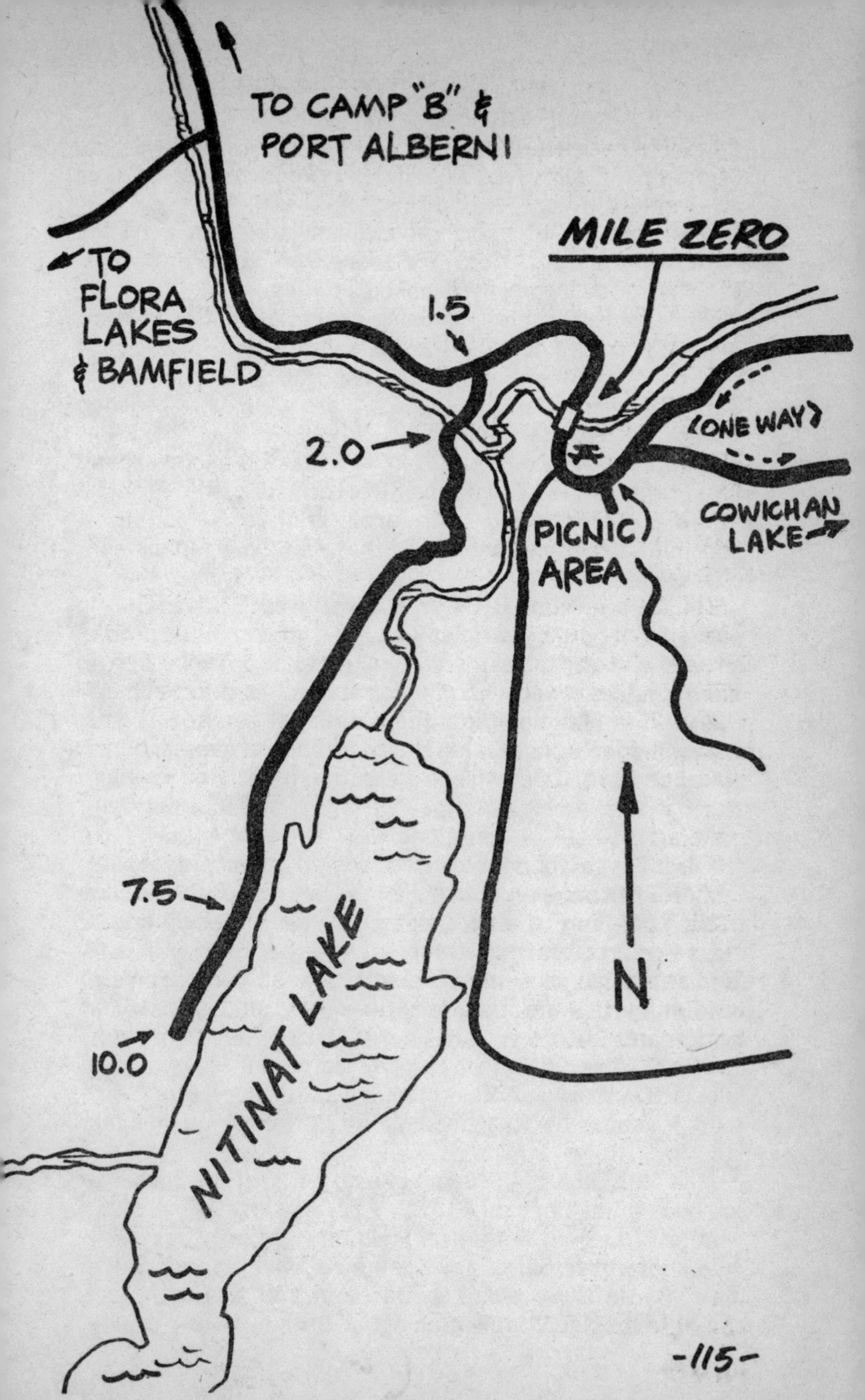

TO CAMP "B" &
PORT ALBERNI

TO
FLORA
LAKES
& BAMFIELD

MILE ZERO

1.5

2.0

⟨ONE WAY⟩

COWICHAN
LAKE

PICNIC
AREA

7.5

10.0

NITINAT LAKE

N

MACMILLAN BLOEDEL PROVIDES
WILDERNESS CAMPING SPOTS

MacMillan Bloedel has provided some wilderness type camping and picnic areas besides several fishing lakes in its Franklin River - Nitinat logging areas.

We found six of these recreational areas on a trip to Bamfield and Poett Nook and there were some other not-yet-developed spots that looked inviting.

There were three picnic-fishing spots along Sarita Lake, two of them with handy places to launch boats.

There are several ways to enter the Nitinat-Franklin-Bamfield recreation logging road area - from Cowichan Lake and from Port Alberni.

We go in from Cowichan Lake and make the loop around the Flora-Central South mainline and out the Franklin Camp B access road, with exploration of a couple of shortcut active logging roads that can be used in non-operational hours.

Mile Zero (48.4) — Nitinat River Red Bridge. During operational hours you must wait here for a company radio-equipped truck to take you through to Franklin Camp B. The Flora Main we will travel for start of loop to Pachena-Bamfield is only open in non-operational hours. But from Port Alberni through Camp B to Bamfield is open all hours. So is the road via Cowichan Lake to Nitinat Red Bridge.

Mile 1.5 (46.9) — Left along west shore of Nitinat Lake for six miles to Knob Point. (See previous chapter.)

Mile 5.6 (42.8) —Junction. Flora - Central South mainline is active logging, a little shorter, but a little rougher and closed to recreational travel during operational hours. Straight ahead for South Main and Franklin Camp B. We go left for Flora Line and immediately cross Little Nitinat bridge and keep left.

Mile 9.1 (39.3) — Flora Lake. Road on left leads around lake for several wilderness camping spots along tunnel-like road. It is possible to slide small boat through bushes into lake for fishing.

Mile 11.5 (36.9) — Crown Lake on left. Not much chance for boat launching.

Mile 14.1 (34.3) — Central Main on right provides a 5.4-mile shortcut to Sarita Lake camping-fishing spots, Sarita Main, Sarita River along Sarita Main and to Poett Nook campground and boat launching for Barkley Sound fishing.

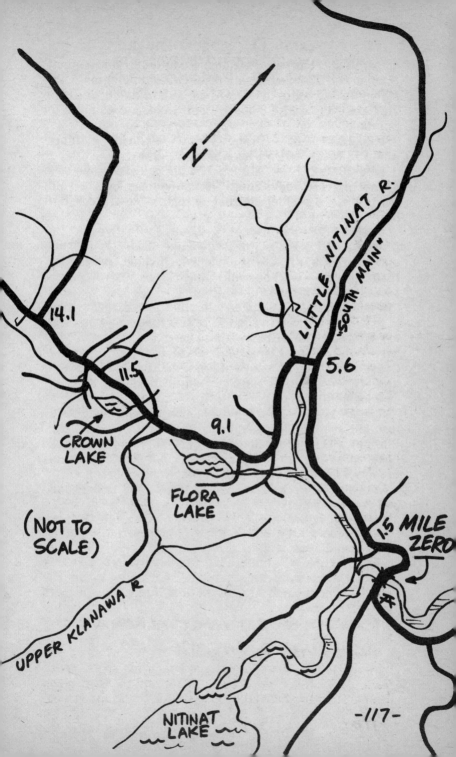

N

14.1

LITTLE NITINAT R.

"SOUTH MAIN"

11.5

5.6

9.1

CROWN LAKE

FLORA LAKE

(NOT TO SCALE)

1.5 MILE ZERO

UPPER KLANAWA R.

NITINAT LAKE

-117-

By this shortcut it is 28.5 miles from Red Bridge to Poett
Nook and 41.2 miles to Bamfield. By continuing on Flora
Main it is 31.1 miles to Poett Nook, 35.8 to Bamfield. To go
via Camp B it is 32.4 miles to Poett Nook and 45 miles to
Bamfield.

Mile 16.4 (32.0) — Branch 265 on left leads to Upper
Klanawa River, but we keep straight ahead.

Mile 20.9 (27.5) — Branch 139 on right is a four-mile
connecting road above South Sarita River and joins up with
Sarita Main ... another alternative road to Poett Nook, but
not a shortcut.

Mile 21.5 (26.9) — Bridge over South Sarita River.

Mile 23.8 (24.6) — Rousseau Lake. There is a small
pullout spot just before the lake which could be used for
roadside picnicking. You could launch small boats from fire
access point off road.

Mile 25.1 (23.3) — Road on left is new active logging road
in to Klanawa River. In the future this road could be used
to get to a spot for a Klanawa base camp to establish a trail
north-south along Klanawa River to connect with West
Coast hiking trail at mouth of Klanawa River ... but at the
time of writing this wasn't being considered in park
development plans.

Mile 26.6 (21.8) — After driving alongside Pachena Lake
turn left at top of lake for Pachena Beach and Bamfield.
Straight ahead goes alongside east shore of Frederick
Lake, past a camping-picnicking spot on shores of
Frederick Lake and on to Sarita-Poett Nook - Albernis.

At this point we will turn left for a side trip to Pachena
Beach - Bamfield.

(SARITA-POETT NOOK-ALBERNIS
CONTINUED ON PAGE 130.)

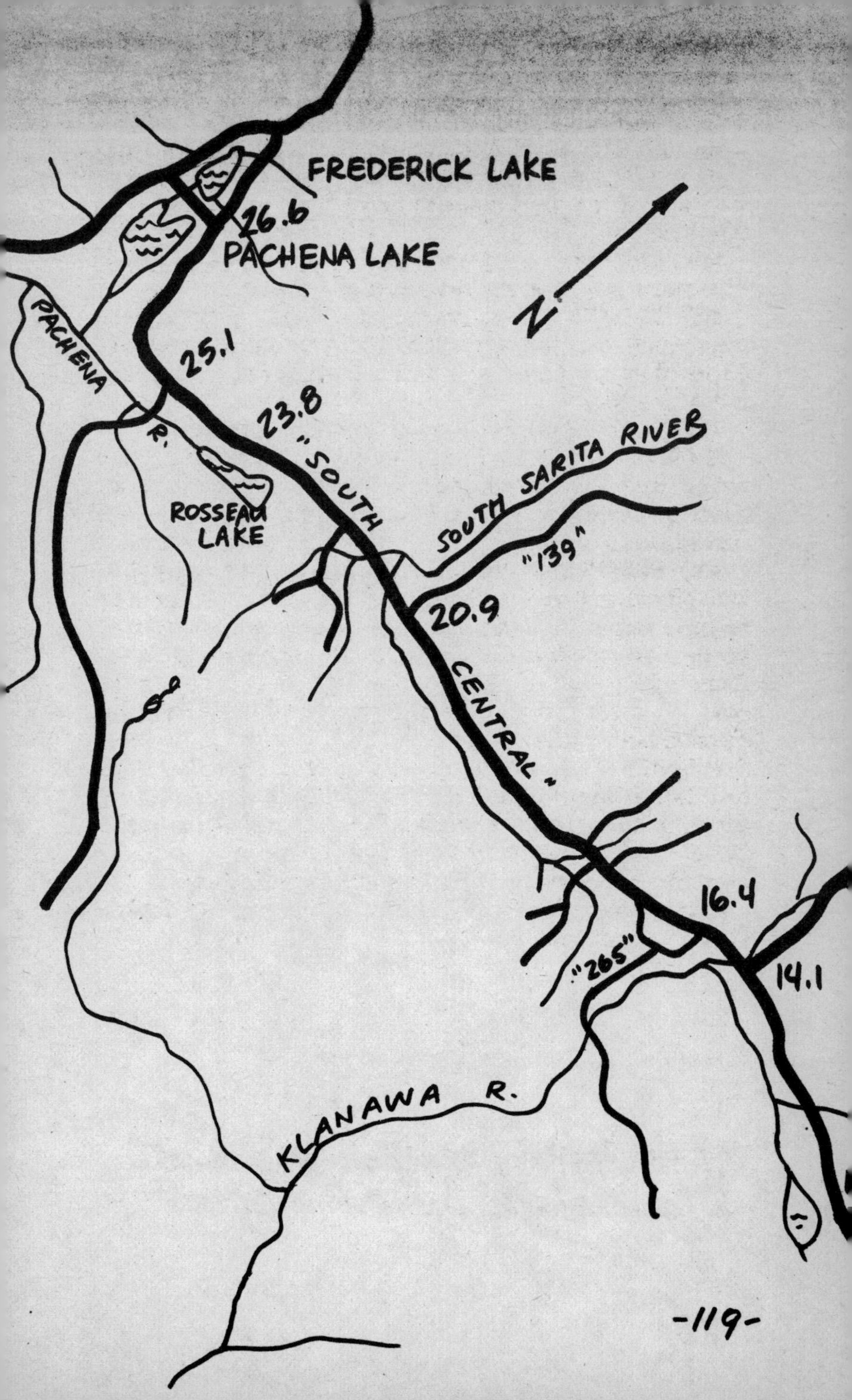

FREDERICK LAKE

26.6
PACHENA LAKE

25.1

23.8

PACHENA R.

ROSSEAU
LAKE

"SOUTH

SOUTH SARITA RIVER

"139"

20.9

"CENTRAL"

16.4

"265"

14.1

KLANAWA R.

Youngsters enjoy getting out in the forests. This is MacMillan - B.C. forest service campground at head of Nitinat Lake.

Canoers Ron Jones and Roger Spurling enjoy trip down Nitinat River and eventually into Nitinat Triangle lake system.

Pachena Beach from West Coast Trail.

Pachena Lake gives up trout to anglers fishing from shore.

WEST COAST TRAIL
STARTS AT PACHENA
...OCEAN FISHING FROM BAMFIELD

You don't really have to be an enthusiastic hiker or a young person to enjoy at least part of the West Coast Trail in Pacific Rim National Park.

The easiest way is to take an enjoyable weekend and camp at Pachena Beach, where the Ohiaht Indian Band operates Anacla Park campground, bordering the Pachena River estuary and beautiful sandy Pachena Beach, which is something like a miniature Long Beach.

This campground is the starting point for the western end of the West Coast Trail and the first four or five miles of trail, out to Pachena Lighthouse on the Pacific Coast, is an enjoyable and easy hike along a fine trail.

It is after Pachena Lighthouse the trail starts to get a little rough and sometimes very rough.

The first four or five miles is the easiest and most popular part of the trail for obvious reasons. It is a comfortable day hike - there and back - from the campground and pretty well anyone, from grandmother to little toddlers can make it.

Thousands who visit the West Coast Trail each summer go no further than the lighthouse.

Others who haven't the time, or the stamina, to make the whole rugged 45-mile trail hike, often go as far as they can in one day, maybe two days, and then hike back again.

Pachena Beach is an ideal family base camp.

The campground skirts the beach with a buffer of logs and beautiful tall trees sheltering campers from the coastal winds.

There are pit toilets and you can get water from the band store at the entrance to the camp. There is no sani-station for campers with holding tanks as yet, so be sure to arrive with an empty holding tank.

There is almost unlimited camping room and the band has big plans for improvements under direction of National Parks experts.

Start of the trail is through the Ross Bible camp at the eastern end of the Indian campground and there is an information hut and registration point as you reach the start of the trail, a hundred yards on.

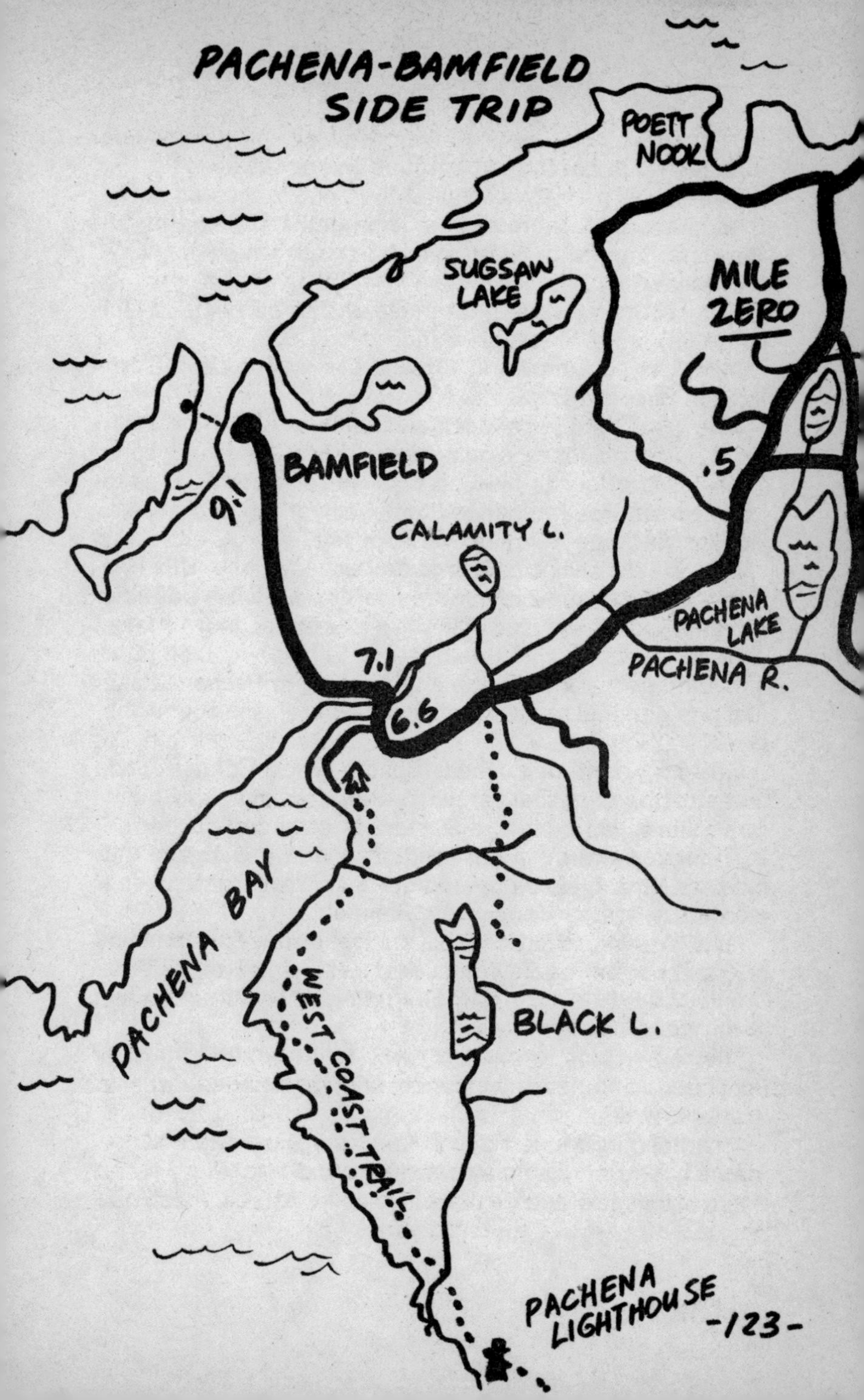

PACHENA-BAMFIELD SIDE TRIP

POETT NOOK

SUGSAW LAKE

MILE ZERO

.5

BAMFIELD

9¹

CALAMITY L.

PACHENA LAKE

PACHENA R.

7.1

6.6

PACHENA BAY

WEST COAST TRAIL

BLACK L.

PACHENA LIGHTHOUSE

Those who don't want to hike the trail can have a fine outdoor holiday at the campground and on the beach.

Bamfield is really two communities, one at the end of the road on the east shore of Bamfield Inlet, and the other on the west shore, with its unique boardwalk, which may only be reached by boat.

To visit the far side of Bamfield and Cape Beale is just like being on a different island.

Mile Zero — Junction at top end of Pachena Lake. Turn left for Pachena-Bamfield.

Mile .5 — Right goes along west side of Frederick Lake for .5 miles to a lovely picnic-camping-boat launching spot, with room for four or five campers, and another .8 miles to junction with road to Sarita-Poett Nook at top end of lake. But for Pachena-Bamfield we turn left.

Mile .7 — Left for picnic area on Pachena Lake. This is a side road for a couple of hundred yards where it is possible to camp alongside road. There is a path leading to lake, with pit toilets. It would be possible to hump a small punt along the path. There is some fair fishing in Pachena Lake and it is possible to fish from the logging slash around the lake.

Mile 6.6 — Left for Pachena Beach, Anacla Campground and start of west coast trail. It is quarter mile to Ohiaht Band store, gas pumps, and start of campground beside Sarita River and beautiful sandy Pachena Beach, and 1.3 miles to Ross bible camp and start of West Coast hiking trail. Keep straight ahead for Bamfield.

Mile 7.1 — Cross Pachena River. Foot bridge beside main bridge is part of the old West Coast Lifesaving Trail.

Mile 9.1 — Left for Ostrom's machine shop, gas and beach boat launching.

Mile 9.2 — Left for boat rentals. Right for half mile to Port Desire and new boat launching ramp and tieup wharf, with plenty of parking space and sheltered cove for tieup before heading for Barkley Sound fishing waters.

Mile 9.5 — Bamfield picnic park at end of road.

End of side trip. Back to Mile 26.6 on loop travel.

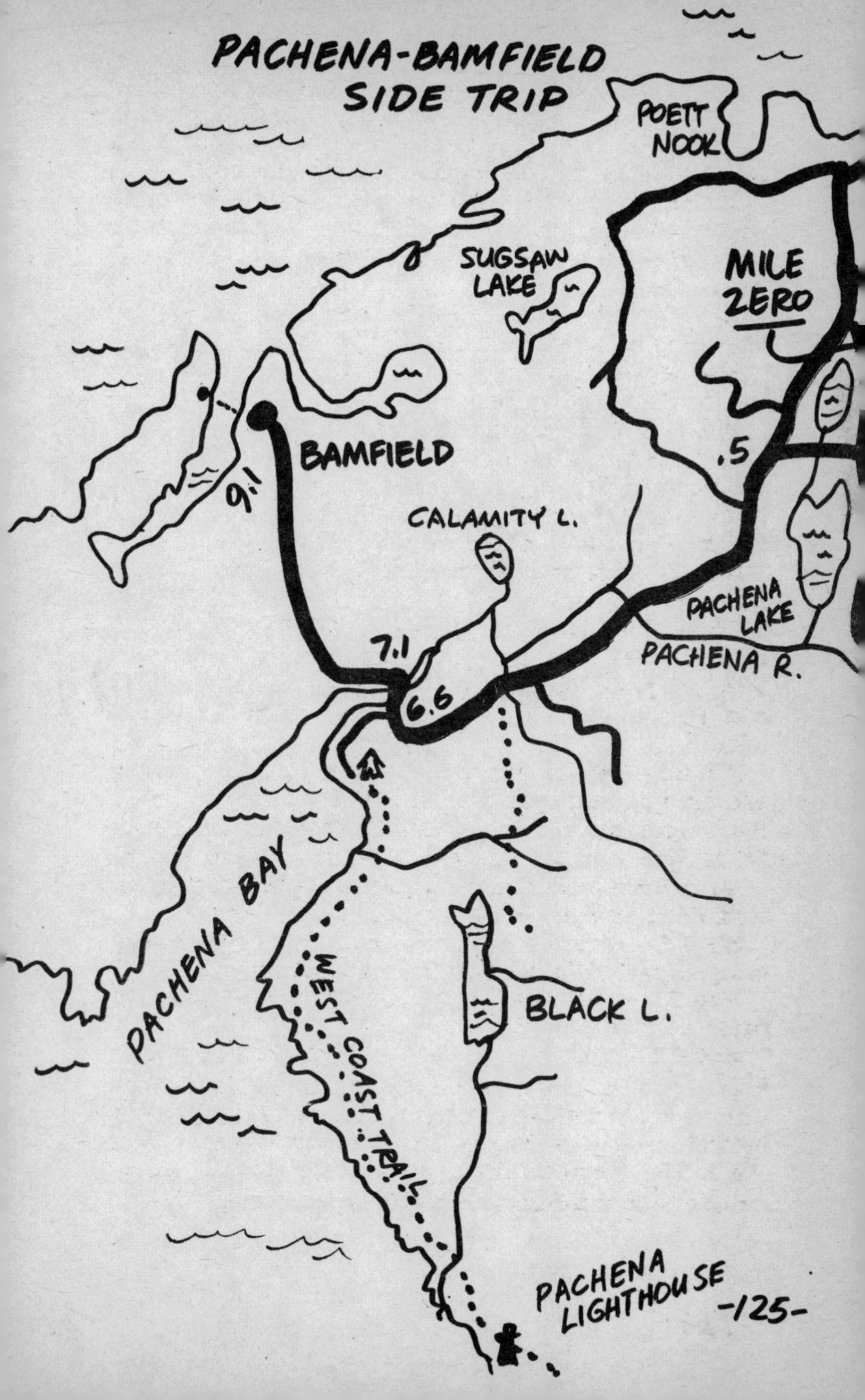

PACHENA-BAMFIELD
SIDE TRIP

POETT NOOK

SUGSAW LAKE

MILE ZERO

BAMFIELD

9.1

.5

CALAMITY L.

PACHENA LAKE

7.1

PACHENA R.

6.6

PACHENA BAY

BLACK L.

WEST COAST TRAIL

PACHENA LIGHTHOUSE

BARKLEY SOUND
FOR FISHING, CRUISING

Barkley Sound, with its 100 or so comparatively little known wilderness islands and inlets, provides cruising and fishing waters comparable to the Gulf Islands in the Gulf of Georgia.

You can trailer your boat over logging roads to Bamfield and Poett Nook to launch for fishing and cruising in these fascinating waters, some of which is in the Pacific Rim National Park.

At Bamfield there is a rough beach launching spot for small boats besides Ostrom's machine shop, and there is a first class launch ramp, small boat wharf and parking area at Port Desire, a fully sheltered, almost fully enclosed bay adjacent to Bamfield.

It is reached by a short (about a quarter mile) road opposite the Bamfield government wharf and boat rental facilities.

Poett Nook, where there is a privately-operated campground and boat launching and wharf facilities, is another nearby sheltered and almost fully enclosed cove. It opens directly into the Sarita Bay tyee fishing waters.

Poett Nook is about half a mile beyond the junction at Sarita.

You don't have to go far to fish, but it is great fun to explore around the islands within 12 or 15 miles of Poett Nook and Bamfield.

How lovely these windswept rugged islands and islets are. Their rock walls have been sculptured by the wind and ocean surf and feature caves, tunnels and holes-in-the-wall spectaculars.

Some were once inhabited as summer camps for Indians and there are still meadows to be seen. Others are too small for human dwellings. None are occupied now. This is the last remaining stronghold of the bald eagle. If you see an eagle in a tree you can be sure you will find fish nearby.

When you are in the Effingham group you are about 12 miles, or half an hour cruising time, from Poett Nook or Bamfield.

But, that is only a small part of the cruising water available. You can whip across to Ucluelet, to Toquart Bay, Holford Bay, Kildonan, Fatty Basin, San Mateo, and a score of other fascinating places

These waters can get rough, but mostly they are sheltered and there are plenty of places to duck for cover.

There is good winter chinook fishing out of Poett Nook in January, February and March, and sometimes the fish come right into the cove. May to mid-June is good for 18 to 30-pounders off Kirby Point and the Effingham Islands. Coho come in July, but at first they mostly stay on the outside off Cree Island and beyond the Effinghams and Cape Beale. August through September is the time for the big tyee, all the way to the head of Alberni Inlet.

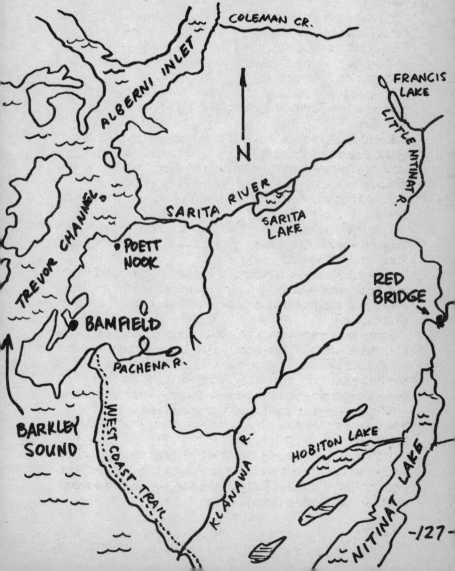

COLEMAN CR.

ALBERNI INLET

FRANCIS LAKE

LITTLE NITINAT R.

N

SARITA RIVER

SARITA LAKE

TREVOR CHANNEL

POETT NOOK

RED BRIDGE

BAMFIELD

PACHENA R.

BARKLEY SOUND

WEST COAST TRAIL

KLANAWA R.

HOBITON LAKE

NITINAT LAKE

Barkley Sound and adjacent waters is known as the
Graveyard of the Pacific. This is the wreck of the
Vanlene.

Sarita Bay where angler spin-fished off rocks for salmon
which were jumping all over bay.

Sports fishermen and campers have found isolated Poett
Nook at Sarita, near Bamfield.

Mile 26.6 (21.8) — Junction with Bamfield — Pachena Road and we keep straight ahead along the east shore of Frederick Lake for Poett Nook.

Mile 27.2 (21.2) — Left goes to lakeshore picnic-camping spot.

Mile 27.6 (20.8) — Upper junction at top end of Frederick Lake. When driving from Port Alberni-Sarita direction you keep right on this junction for Bamfield.

Mile 29.6 (18.8) — Sarita River log dump. Right for Franklin-Alberni. For Poett Nook turn left for three-tenths mile, then left up hill for four-tenths mile for beautiful anchorage, boat launching and privately operated campground and marina. This is the gateway to Barkley Sound - Sarita Bay salmon fishing waters and where to find the big tyee salmon in September-October.

We turn right for Camp B and follow along Sarita Bay at mouth of river where in October-November you can spinfish for salmon from shore.

Mile 29.8 (18.6) — Could launch cartopper from beach, but there is a proper ramp at nearby Poett Nook.

Mile 30.6 (17.8) — Boundary of Indian Reserve property.

Mile 30.8 (17.6) — Beach and rocks where anglers cast for salmon in Sarita Bay.

Mile 31.2 (17.2) — Sarita River mouth.

SARITA RIVER, LAKE
FOR CAMPING - FISHING

Mile 32.7 (15.7) — Indian Reserve boundary.

Mile 33.1 (15.3) — Cross small bridge. There are numerous pullout spots and river access points for fishermen.

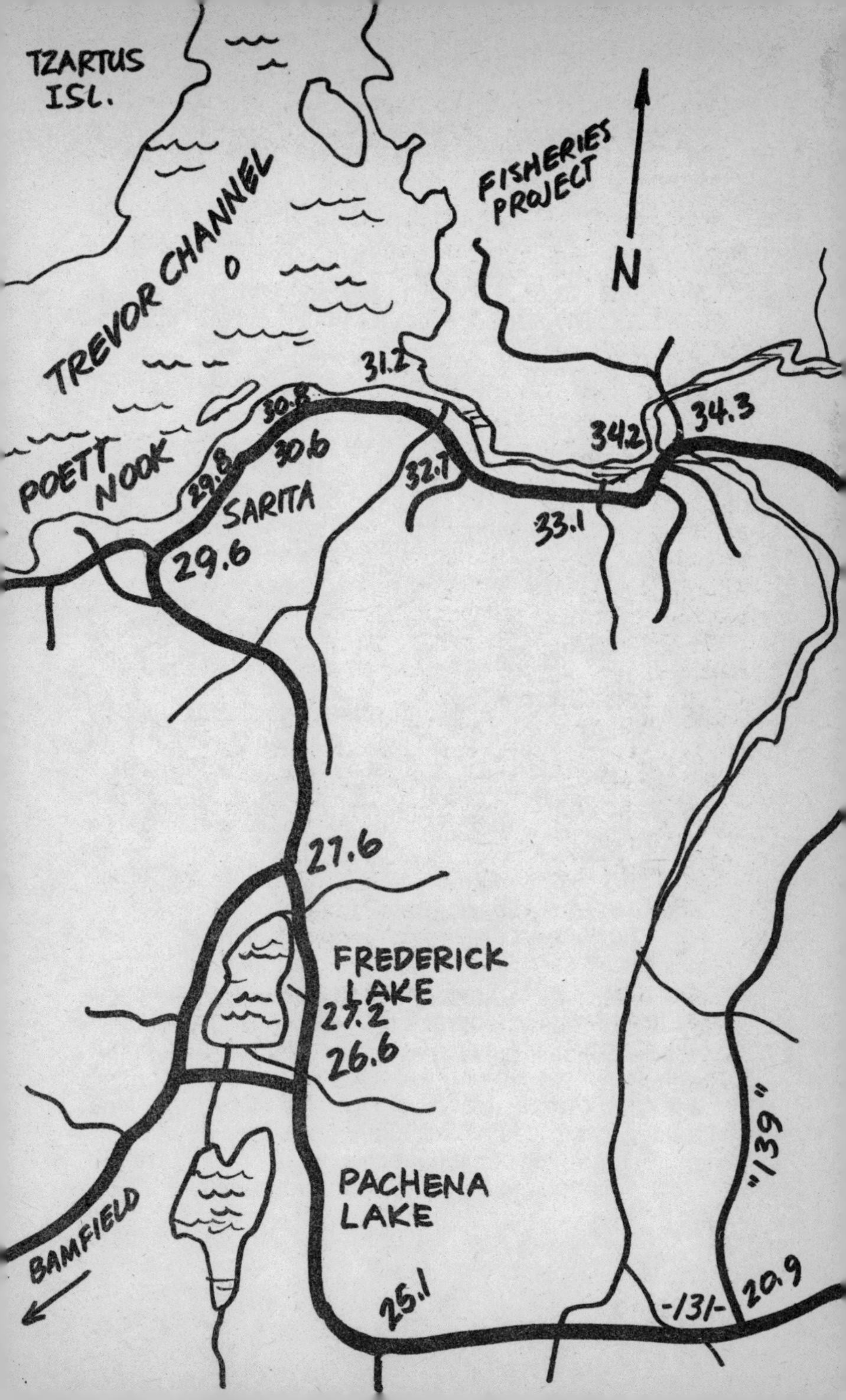
TZARTUS ISL.
TREVOR CHANNEL
FISHERIES PROJECT
N
31.2
30.8
30.6
29.8
POETT NOOK
32.7
34.2
34.3
33.1
SARITA
29.6
27.6
FREDERICK LAKE
27.2
26.6
PACHENA LAKE
"139"
BAMFIELD
25.1
-131-
20.9

Mile 34.2 (14.2) — Bridge over Sarita River. This is where big tyee salmon spawn. There is a place on either side where steelheaders could park.

Mile 34.3 (14.1) — Blenheim Main on left. This also goes to federal fisheries Coronation Creek experiment, in conjunction with logging company.

Mile 36.8 (11.6) — Branch 139 on right. This follows South Sarita River to connect up with South Flora mainline at Mile 20.9 mark.

Mile 37.9 (10.5) — Cross bridge and then spur road on right.

Mile 38.3 (10.1) — Branch road on right, non-active.

Mile 38.5 (9.9) — First of three (on left) Sarita Lake picnic sites provided by MB. This is in open and has been a favorite for some years. If you put your boat in the lake and go to the west end you will find a rough walking trail that will take you to spectacular falls.

Mile 39.2 (9.2) — Second picnic site. This is a rather big area with room for five or six different camper units and access to the beachfront. These picnic spots are not serviced in the winter.

Mile 39.7 (8.7) — Third campsite on left. This is the only one of the three with proper camping units, but it isn't right on lake. Others are really supposed to be for picnics. On right across from campground is Central Main which provides the shortcut for 5.4 miles to join Flora main at the 14.1-mile mark.

Mile 39.8 (8.6) — Cross small bridge.

Mile 40.5 (7.9) — Logging spur enters on right.

Mile 41.0 (7.4) — Logging spur enters on right.

Mile 41.1 (7.3) — Cross bridge over Sarita River.

Mile 41.2 (7.2) — Spencer Main enters on left and is active line leading to Alberni Inlet at at least two points.

Mile 42.6 (5.8) — A major logging road enters on left, but it really doesn't go anywhere except to logging spurs.

Mile 48.4 (Zero) — Travel up a long hill and down a long hill, along rather dull road, until you reach junction at Camp. B. Right goes to Nitinat country again and straight ahead through camp and left leads to Albernis.

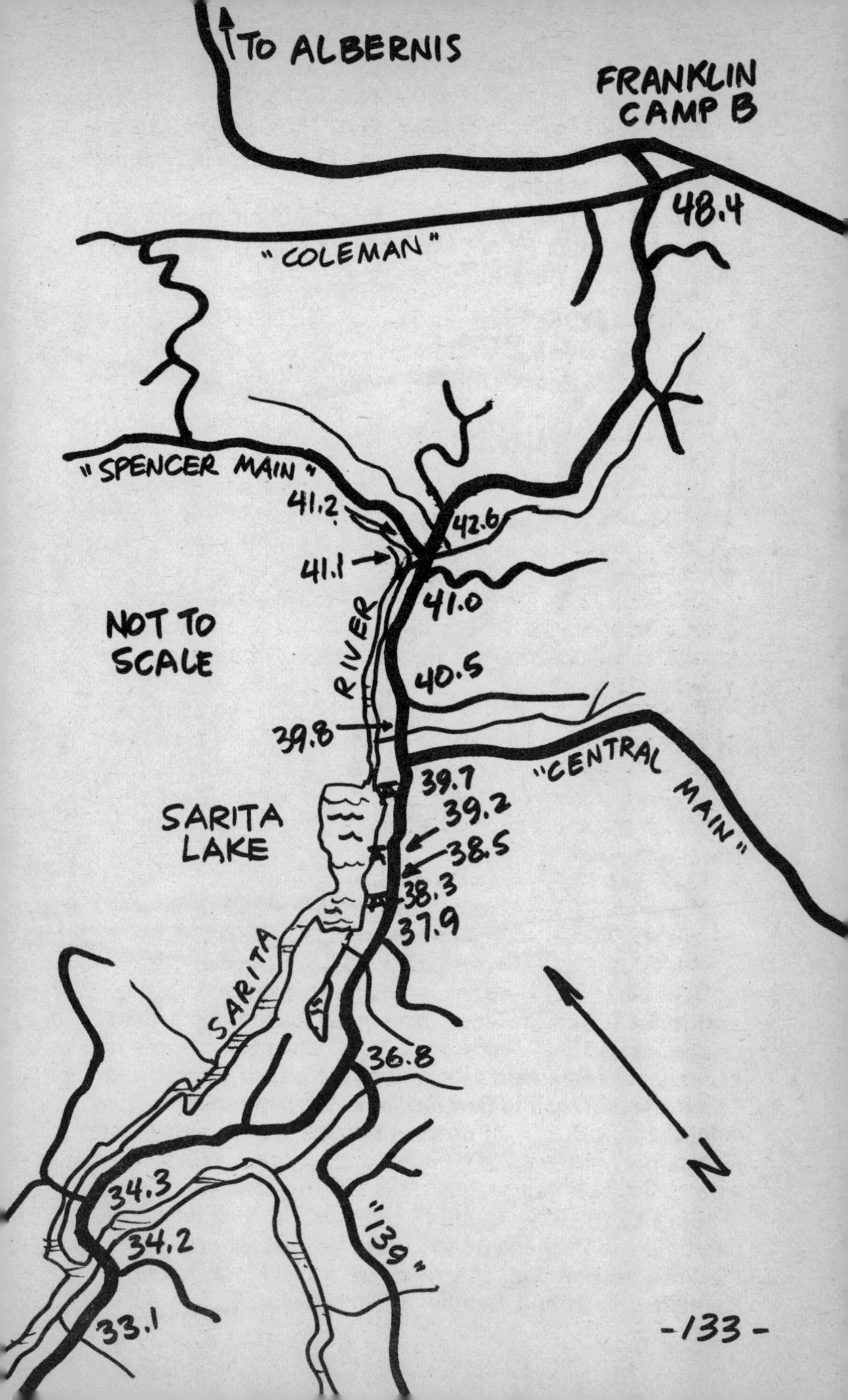

TO ALBERNIS

FRANKLIN
CAMP B

48.4

"COLEMAN"

"SPENCER MAIN"

41.2

42.6

41.1

41.0

RIVER

NOT TO
SCALE

40.5

39.8

39.7

39.2

38.5

"CENTRAL MAIN"

SARITA
LAKE

38.3

37.9

SARITA

36.8

N

34.3

34.2

"139"

33.1

NITINAT RIVER TO ALBERNI
...AND BIG TYEE SALMON

Mile Zero (44.6) — Nitinat River red bridge. During operating hours wait at bridge for radio-controlled vehicle which you can follow.

Mile 1.5 (43.1) — Junction. Left for Hobiton, Knob Point. Straight ahead for Flora Lake - Port Alberni. We go straight ahead for Port Alberni.

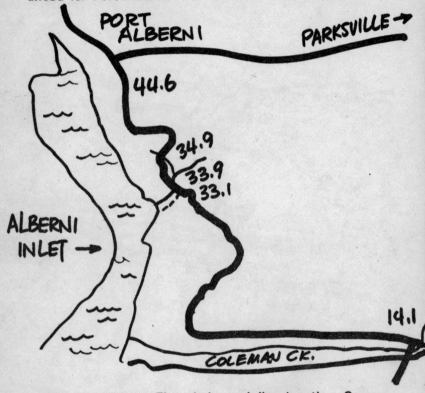

Mile 5.6 (39.0) — Flora Lake mainline junction. Cross bridge on left for Flora Lake and alternative route to Pachena and Bamfield. We go straight ahead this time for Camp B., main road to Bamfield and Port Alberni.

Mile 11.4 (33.2) — Francis Lake for trout fishing and picnicking.

Mile 14.1 (30.5) — Camp B. intersection. Left for Sarita, Bamfield and Pachena Beach. Right for Port Alberni. This is the intersection we returned to from Flora mainline, Pachena Beach and Bamfield.

Mile 33.1 (11.5) — China Creek Park. Turn left for campground and boat launching for Alberni Inlet tyee fishing. Straight ahead for Port Alberni.

Mile 33.9 (10.7) — China Creek bridge and steelhead pool.

Mile 34.9 (9.7) — MB Cameron camp.

Mile 44.6 (Zero) — Enter Port Alberni and paved roads.

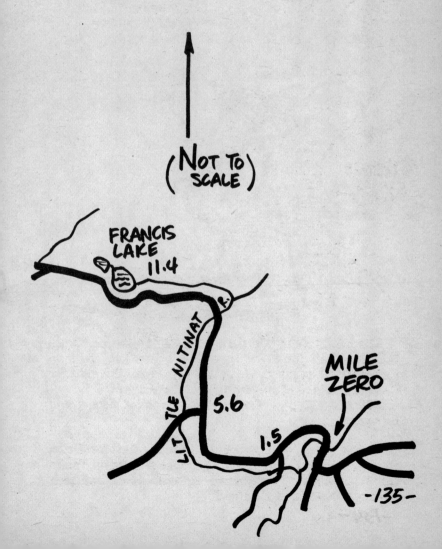

LAKE-STUDDED CIRCLE TRIP
FROM GREAT CENTRAL LAKE

North of Great Central Lake a network of logging roads in the Ash River division of MacMillan Bloedel operations leads to fine hunting areas, attractive fishing spots, and beautiful scenery.

A 45-mile circle trip will take you to several lakes, along the Stamp River, alongside three different sections of the Ash River and within striking distance of many more attractive spots.

When you reach the headwaters of the Ash River at the far end of the circle drive you will have actually penetrated by road into the southeast corner of Strathcona Park.

If you continue on the road seven more miles you would

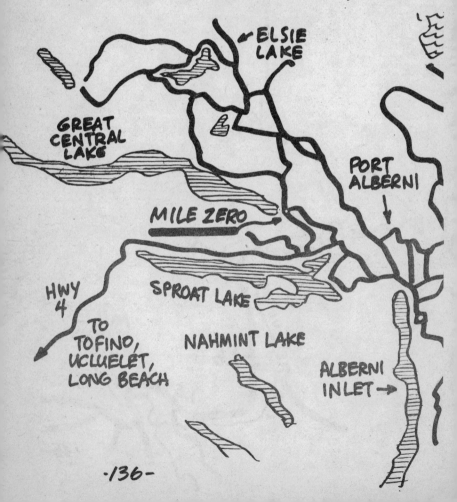

come to Oshinow (sometimes called Deep) Lake, a large lake within the park, which may be reached by car and fished for cutthroat either by boat or from shore.

This lake is 1,380 feet above sea level and the head-waters of the Ash River run into it from Tzela Lake, to the north, which is one of the favorite camping spots for hikers on the Strathcona Park mountain-top ridge trail.

This logging road trip starts at Great Central Lake, just 13 1/2 miles from the junction road at Alberni.

At Great Central Lake, just before reaching the Ark Resort, turn right, onto the logging road. MacMillan Bloedel's Sproat Lake Division Map is the one to follow.

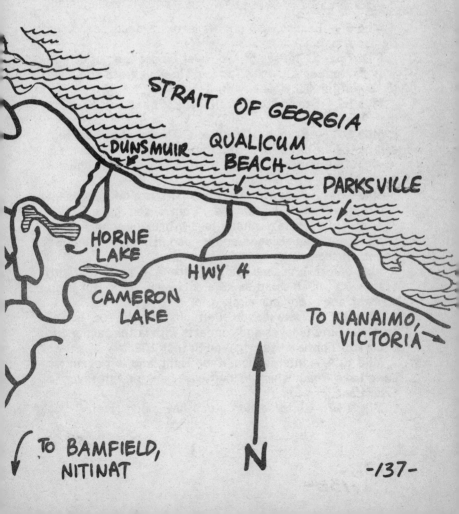

Since the first edition of this book MB has signed this intricate road network and provided primitive camping and boat launching sites.

Mile Zero — Gate at bridge over Stamp River where it empties from Great Central Lake. There is fine trout fishing right there.

Mile .4 — Dam on Stamp River.

Mile .9 — Upper Stamp Falls. There is some fine steelheading and trout fishing on Stamp River, in both winter and summer.

Mile 1.2 — Thunder Bay Road on left. Keep right on main road.

Mile 6 — Branch 100 on left leads to dead end. Keep right on mainline road.

Mile 7.5 — Glimpses of Ash River before it empties into Stamp. Stop car and walk 100 feet through grass and bush for beautiful sight of falls on Ash River.

Mile 7.7 — Branch 101 on left leads to dead end. Keep on mainline.

Mile 8.3 — Branch 102 on left. This is the road that completes the circle later, and the road for quickest access to beautiful fishing lakes. But we keep on mainline for circle tour.

Mile 8.5 — Bridge over Ash River. This is a beautiful spot where the Ash River empties from Dixon Lake, which appears to be an ideal canoing lake with many small fingers like a spider, small islands, and is good fishing for rainbows and cutthroats from shore or a boat.

Just before crossing bridge there is a road to right, branch 73, which could make a circle trip back. But keep straight ahead for our circle trip.

Mile 9.8 — Intersection. Left on Branch 108 is yet another route to lakes and connects with latter part of our circle trip. For now keep right on Branch 103.

Mile 11.4 — Intersection. Keep right, and left again for Long Lake Road, which follows east bank of Ash River to Elsie Lake.

Mile 13.7 — Intersection. Keep left, along river.

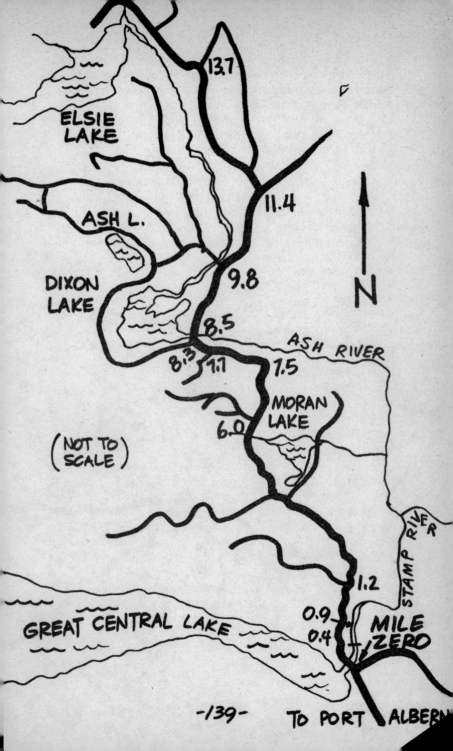

ELSIE LAKE

13.7

11.4

ASH L.

9.8

DIXON LAKE

8.5

ASH RIVER

8.3 7.7 7.5

MORAN LAKE

6.0

N

(NOT TO SCALE)

STAMP RIVER

1.2

0.9

0.4

GREAT CENTRAL LAKE

MILE ZERO

-139-

TO PORT ALBERNI

Mile 16.1 — First sight of Elsie Lake, and hydro dam. It is a pitiful sight, a sea of tree stumps, but much better than a bunch of dead trees sticking out of the lake at high water.

Elsie Lake is a big lake, several miles long at the 1,050-foot level. It provides some excellent fishing for both cutthroat and rainbow trout in the fall and in the spring just after the ice melts.

Mile 16.7 — Cross stream on north side of Elsie Lake. You could launch cartoppers in this area.

Mile 18.2 — After following the lake, come to an intersection just before crossing Ramsay Creek. The road to right leads to Long Lake and if you turn left at first intersection another road follows Ramsay Creek past small lakes to Oshinow Lake. For circle drive keep straight ahead along Elsie Lake.

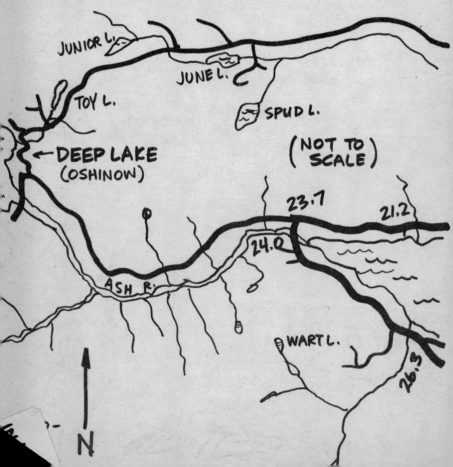

Mile 21.2 — Road on left acts as launching ramp to Elsie Lake.

Mile 23.7 — Straight ahead goes to Oshinow Lake. For circle trip turn left, down steep hill. The road along Elsie Lake can be rough. Now you are in Strathcona Park and heading down hill to Ash River.

Mile 24 — Bridge over Ash River, pretty falls on one side, deep pools on the other. You now head back for last half of circle tour.

Mile 26.3 — Junction. Keep right. You now leave Elsie Lake and get to better roads.

Mile 27.5 — From top of hill a beautiful view of Lois, McLaughlan and Ash Lakes, all of which produce cutthroats and rainbows.

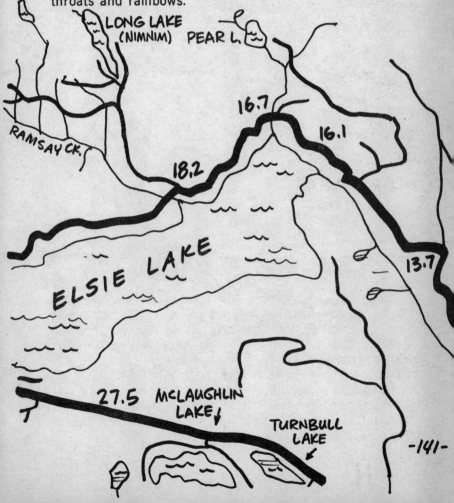

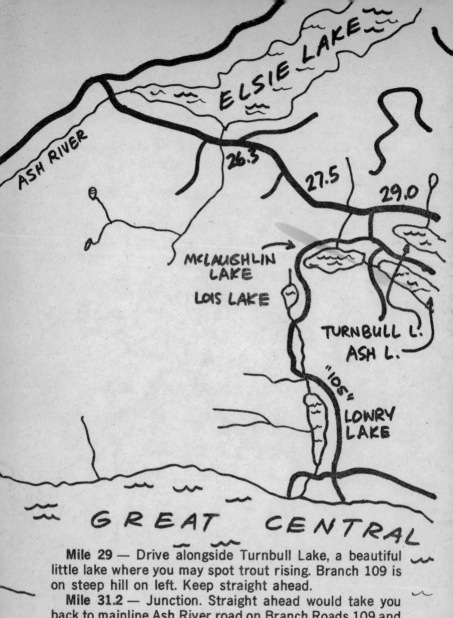

Mile 29 — Drive alongside Turnbull Lake, a beautiful little lake where you may spot trout rising. Branch 109 is on steep hill on left. Keep straight ahead.

Mile 31.2 — Junction. Straight ahead would take you back to mainline Ash River road on Branch Roads 109 and 108. We turn right to Branch 102.

Mile 31.6 — Junction. Right up 105 goes to Ash Lake, McLaughlan Lake, Lois Lake, Lowry Lake and deadends at Great Central Lake. We will keep straight ahead on Branch 102, past foot of Ash Lake, a medium-sized lake.

Mile 31.9 — Bridge over little creek.

Mile 32.2 — Dixon Lake comes in sight, where Ash River flows into it.

Mile 34.9 — Junction with 102 and Ash River mainline. This is the end of the circle.

Mile 43.1 — Back at logging gate and on to government road again at Great Central Lake.

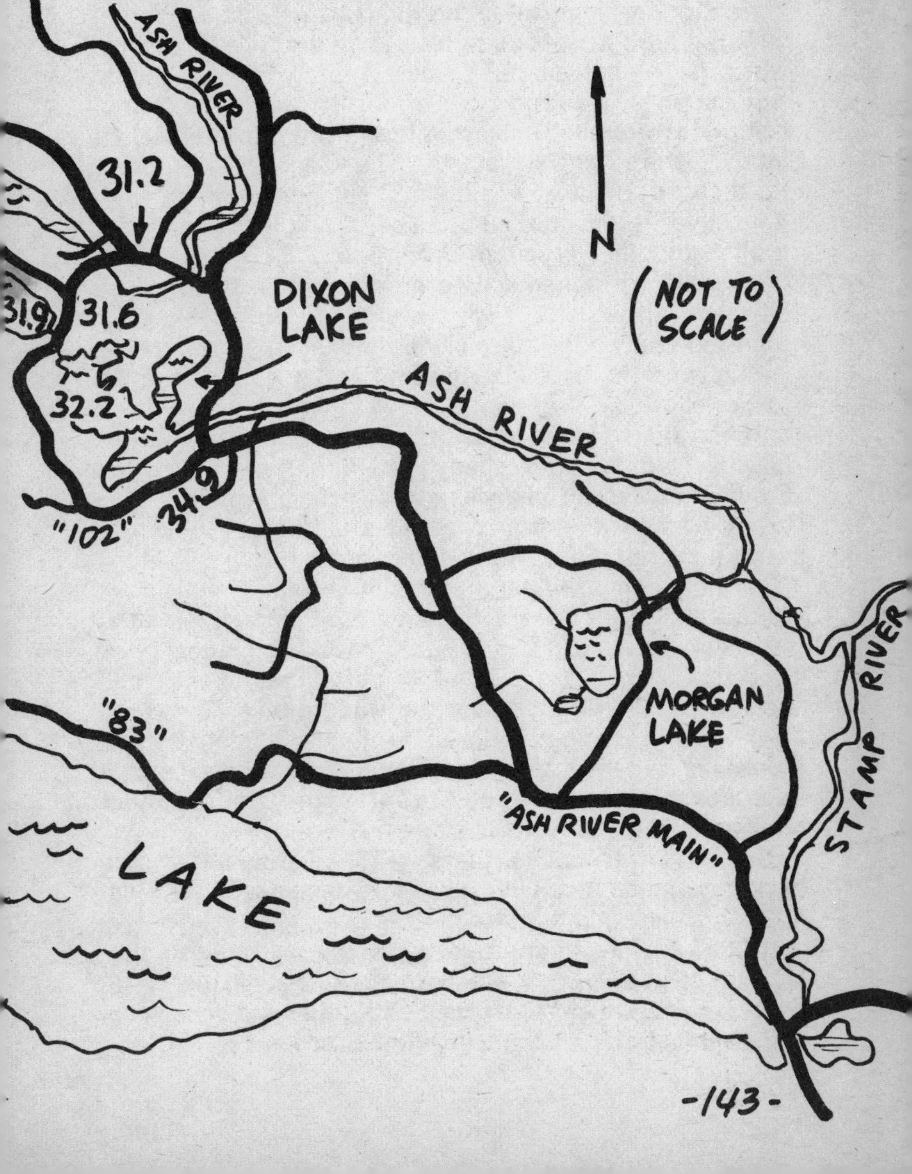

N

(NOT TO SCALE)

ASH RIVER

31.2

31.9 31.6

32.2

DIXON LAKE

ASH RIVER

"102" 34.9

MORGAN LAKE

"83"

"ASH RIVER MAIN"

LAKE

STAMP RIVER

NAHMINT WATERSHED
BLUEPRINT FOR FUTURE

MacMillan Bloedel logging roads at the start of 1975 stretched down the west shore of Alberni Inlet, 3 1/2 miles beyond Macktush Creek and within a half mile of Nahmint Bay ... and they had started creeping further into the Nahmint watershed.

Further development in the Nahmint watershed awaited an integrated multiple use plan for the entire watershed, which is being prepared by all resource users.

It marks a new approach in British Columbia, with a complete watershed subjected to a full integrated resource study before logging starts. The Toquart watershed, northeast of Ucluelet was the first complete watershed on Vancouver Island studied by all users and is being used as a pilot for other resource use studies.

Logging was scheduled to go on as scheduled in the adjacent Macktush Creek watershed because the integrated study does not include the Macktush watershed.

But, even there, stringent new forestry guidelines were to be followed.

The Nahmint watershed will be a pattern for future logging in other watersheds, and a pattern for British Columbia's second chance, when second growth timber grows of sufficient size to be merchantable.

We must not repeat the mistakes of the past.

In the Nahmint watershed resource users — fish and wildlife biologists, federal fisheries, park planners, forestry officials, water resource experts, company planners and foresters, and others — have made studies of their particular problems concerning the wilderness.

Nahmint watershed is the home of Alberni Inlet's biggest tyee runs, to say nothing of steelhead, trout and game. It is also home for some of the finest timber stands on Vancouver Island.

Under resource use planning important spawning areas have been noted and management objective will be to maintain fish habitat, protect stream bank vegetation, water temperatures and siltation. No logs, fill, obstructions or debris likely to cause pollution will be allowed to be deposited in streams. There will be restrictions on

Virgin timber starts at Macktush Creek, along the new logging road to Nahmint Valley.

equipment operating in streams and upon the taking of gravel from the streams. Bridges and culverts will be controlled.

Tree cutting will be strictly controlled where there is danger of erosion along water courses.

Recreation areas will be set aside for public use.

Timber harvesting will be based on a system of alternate cut and leave patches designed to reduce the potential for excessive runoffs and sediment load to the various creeks.

Timber patches will be left along roadsides to preserve the esthetics of the area.

Game officials will insist on minimal disturbance to winter feeding areas.

Those are some of the objectives. If this integrated use plan is a success it will pave the way for a more compatible system of logging in the future.

The road down Alberni Inlet over the MB logging roads is already enjoyable, the latter part of it over roads restricted to weekend and holiday non-operational-hours travel.

Our trip started at Mission Road, just after crossing the bridge over the Somass River on the Sproat Lake Road out of Port Alberni.

Mile Zero— Mission Road junction with the Sproat Lake Road. Keep left on to Mission Road.

Mile .4— Junction. Keep left for MB Cous Division roads.

Mile 1.6 — Junction. Left for log dump. Keep right, past machine shops.

Mile 2 — Junction. Stirling Arm road on right follows Sproat Lake south shore for some miles and then swings around to walking trail to top end of Nahmint Lake, but road in can be very rough. We keep left on Cous Creek mainline.

Mile 3.8 — Summit line straight ahead on right. We keep left on Cous line.

Mile 3.9 — Overgrown road on left, but we keep straight ahead and pretty soon road starts to follow headwaters of Cous Creek.

Mile 5.7— Branch 409 on right. Keep straight ahead.

Mile 6.1— Branch 414 on right. Keep straight ahead.

Mile 6.6 — Junction at helicopter landing site. Straight ahead and right is Cous Creek and upper Macktush lines. We keep left, cross over Cous Creek bridge. Cous Creek is a steelheading river in winter. This is the end of all-hours road travel. From now on road is restricted to non-operational hours.

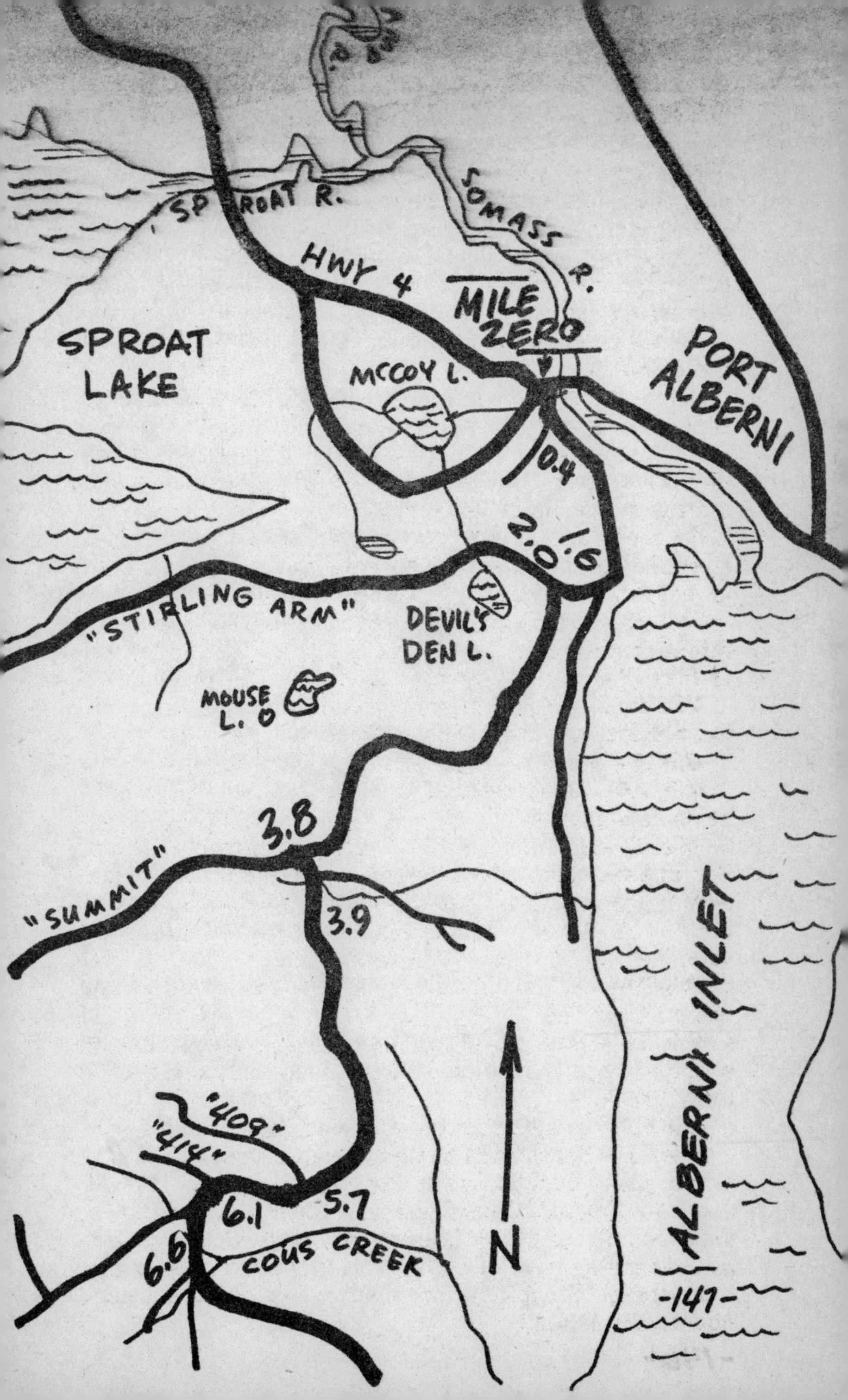

SPROAT R.

SOMASS R.

HWY 4

MILE ZERO

SPROAT LAKE

McCOY L.

PORT ALBERNI

0.4

2.0 1.6

"STIRLING ARM"

DEVIL'S DEN L.

MOUSE L.

3.8

"SUMMIT"

3.9

ALBERNI INLET

"409"

"414"

6.1

5.7

6.6

COUS CREEK

N

-147-

Mile 6.7 — Junction. Uphill on right goes to system of logging spurs and some all hours travel roads. But we keep left and straight ahead on Macktush line.

Mile 9.6 — We get glimpse of Alberni Inlet.

Mile 9.8 — Branch 1150 on right. We keep straight ahead.

Mile 10.6 — Road goes down hill to Alberni Inlet at Stamp Narrows.

Mile 10.8 — Cross small creek and come to mouth at Alberni Inlet.

Mile 11 — Road on right leads to network of spur roads. We keep straight ahead.

Mile 11.1 — Log dump. Could launch small boat. China Creek can be seen on opposite side of Alberni Inlet.

Mile 13.6 — Bridge crosses creek.

Mile 14.2 — Bridge over another creek.

Mile 16.3 — Junction. Branch 2500 and M400 on right. We keep straight ahead over Macktush Creek bridge, which on our trip in late 1974 was the start of virgin timber.

Mile 16.6 — Road to new log dump on left. Straight ahead for Nahmint.

Mile 16.8 — Road skirts Honeymoon Bay, one of the nicest beaches on Alberni Inlet. The log booms will cover one of the finest prawn fishing grounds on the Alberni Inlet, but few people knew about it because the area has been inaccessible except by boat.

The road carried on another 3 1/2 miles to Nahmint Bay and up the valley, but there was blasting and road building ahead and this was as far as we could go on that trip.

Mile by mile, year by year, from now on it will creep further and further into the Nahmint Valley, eventually to truly wilderness Nahmint Lake, but hopefully under an overall plan that will minimize the ravages of logging, yet allow industry to flourish ... and at the same time protect the environment, the wildlife and provide recreational opportunities ... an exciting thought.

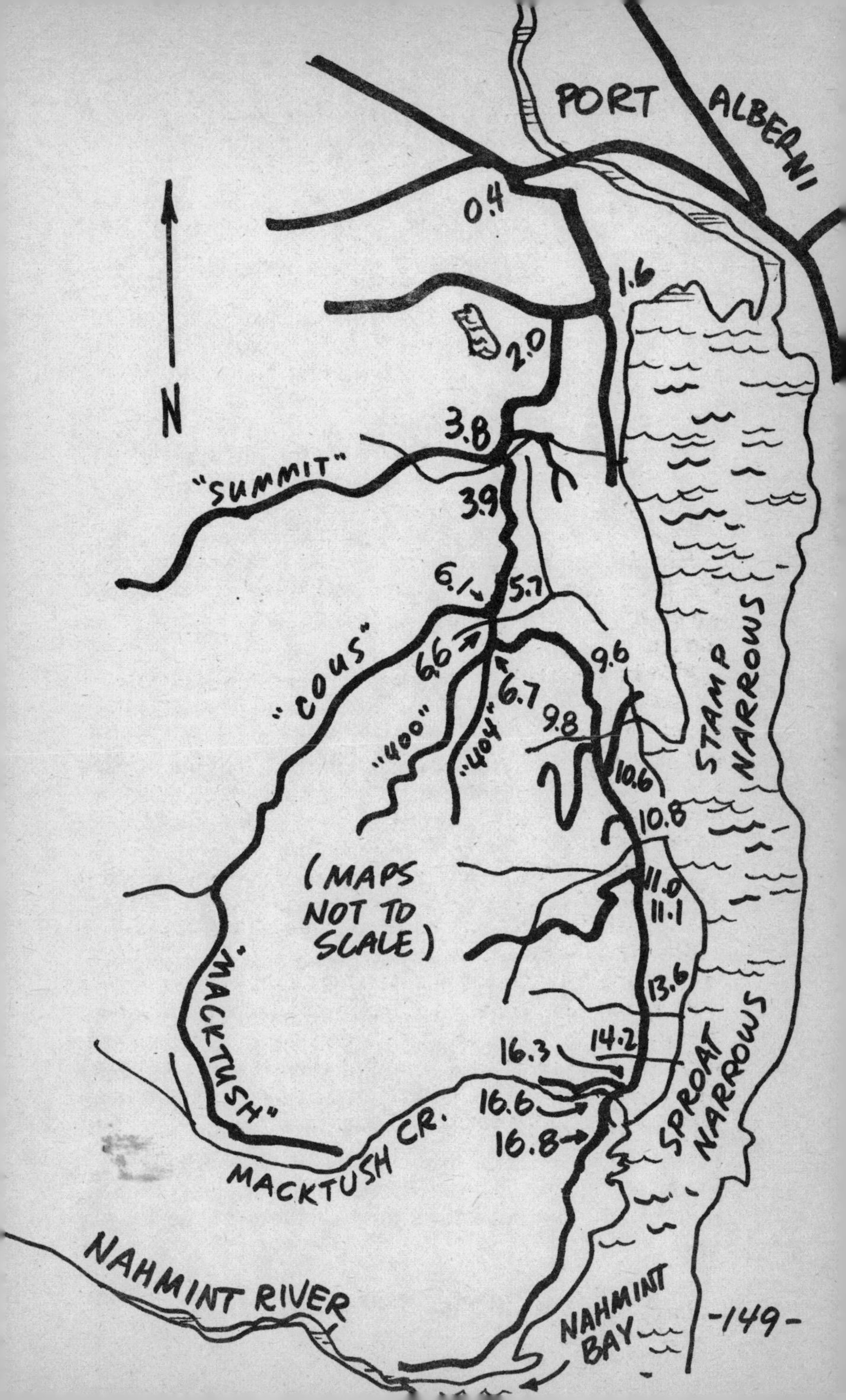

PORT ALBERNI

0.4

1.6

2.0

3.8

3.9

"SUMMIT"

6.1 5.7

"COUS" 6.6

"480" 6.7 9.6

9.8

"404"

10.6

10.8

11.0

11.1

(MAPS
NOT TO
SCALE)

13.6

14.2

16.3

16.6 →

16.8 →

"MACKTUSH"

MACKTUSH CR.

STAMP NARROWS

SPROAT NARROWS

NAHMINT RIVER

NAHMINT BAY

-149-

DRIVE UP MOUNT ARROWSMITH
SKI, FISH AND HIKE

It is now possible to drive up the slopes of Mount Arrowsmith and enjoy lunch almost under the shadow of 5,962 - foot Mount Arrowsmith and its neighboring Mount Cokely.

It is 9.1 miles from the starting point near the summit of the Parksville-Alberni highway to the parking area before the really steep climb, but when we first made the trip in mid-1974 a new three mile bypass road was under construction to provide an easier grade around that hill.

It was 1.7 miles up that steep hill to the Rosseau Chalet where hikers take off to climb Mount Arrowsmith and Mount Cokely.

Another 1.6 miles leads to the turn for Pass 60 spur which leads to a spanking new $225,000 (first stage) ski development which started operating in 1975.

This MacMillan Bloedel Cameron mainline leads into a 1,500 - acre virgin timber mountain playground, which has been acquired by Clayoquot Regional District from MB on a 20-year lease for development as a summer and winter recreational Arrowsmith Mountain Park.

This natural Cokely ski bowl area in the lee of the northwest slopes of seven peaks of Arrowsmith holds some snow all summer and usually provides good skiing conditions from October, through to May and June.

Stage one development provides accommodation for 1,200 skiers a day.

Five year projection is for five lifts with accommodation for 6,500 skiers a day, plus the development of logging roads and trails for cross-country skiing.

The road to the ski area will be an all-weather year-round road, suitable for almost any car.

There is a parking lot for 200 cars at the bottom of a hill about one-mile in along Pass 60 spur and plans called for a day lodge for skiers in winter and hikers in summer.

Plans call for a 3,000-foot Doppelmyr chair lift with a 600-foot vertical drop from Rosseau Ridge, along with a couple of 600-foot rope tows for beginners in the lodge area.

(SEE PHOTO, PAGE 181.)

Longer range plans call for another chair lift to the top of nearly 6,000-foot Mount Cokely.

This Arrowsmith area was popular for skiing in the late 1940s, but it required at least a three-hour hike to reach the ski areas and most skiers started using the easier accessible Green Mountain (CZ Nanaimo Lakes logging roads) and Forbidden Plateau (Courtenay) ski areas.

But now, the accessibility to Arrowsmith by logging roads is changing all that.

Arrowsmith has been popular with hikers for many years and is becoming increasingly so.

Hikers can still take the long way up the trail at Cameron Lake, and that trail follows Pipeline Creek and skirts the new ski bowl.

But now, hikers with less stamina, or less time, can drive to the Rosseau Chalet and take Rosseau Ridge to Cokely Peak and across the saddle to Mount Arrowsmith. Or they can drive to the end of Pass 60 spur and pick up the old Arrowsmith trail from Cameron Lake.

The hike to Cokely from the chalet, which is badly in need of restoration, takes a couple of hours.

Not only hikers and skiers will be able to enjoy Arrowsmith Park.

Just 1-1/2 miles beyond the turn to Pass 60 is some logging slash, through which a short spur leads to St. Mary's Lake which is still (in 1974) almost ringed by virgin timber.

In past years this lake has given up some fine trout fishing, with fish reported to have reached six pounds. You had to hike into it in those days. But since the logging roads reached its shores it hasn't seemed so productive. This is probably one lake that could stand some heavy stocking for recreational fun fishing.

For just plain sightseers the logging road through the area provides some wonderful mountain scenery and also some fine views of the Alberni Valley.

Here is our trip of the Arrowsmith area:

Mile Zero — Turnoff on Alberni side, near top of Parksville - Alberni highway summit. Signs show the way. Left coming from Parksville, right from Alberni. Logging gate few feet in and MB sign welcomes visitors to all-hour travel, with a warning to watch out for heavy vehicles.

Mile 1.7 — Junction at Rogers Creek. Road on right comes five miles from Cameron Division headquarters on Alberni-Bamfield logging road and is another way into the Arrowsmith Mountain Park area. Turn left for Cameron mainline to park.

Mile 3.5— YC main on right. Keep straight ahead, Mount Arrowsmith can now be seen towering above.

Mile 6.1— CM 80 main on right. Keep straight ahead.

Mile 6.3 — River main on right follows south bank of Cameron River. Keep left and cross bridge.

Mile 6.4— CAM 100 spur on left. Keep straight ahead.

Mile 6.6 — Mainline road on right follows north shore of Cameron River for seven miles, almost to Labor Day Lake. Labor Day Lake may also be reached by trail from the CZ Nanaimo Lakes system. For now, keep sharp left up hill for Arrowsmith Mountain Park.

Mile 6.8— Pass 10 spur on right. Keep straight ahead. For next two miles you pass several Pass spur roads on right and left, but keep straight ahead up hill.

Mile 8.6 — Unmarked road on right. It is about here where three-mile road to bypass steep hill will start. That means the mileages given here will become a little outdated until you reach the Rosseau Chalet at our Mile 10.8 mark.

Mile 9.1— Right turn to lower parking lot, straight ahead for steep hill. From parking lot you get glimpses of the frightening hill, which really looked worse than it was. Parking lot also gives good view of Arrowsmith in one direction and Alberni Valley in the other.

Mile 9.6— Start of steepest part of hill.

Mile 10.8— Rosseau Chalet. Fine views of Alberni Valley and west slopes of Cokely and Arrowsmith. This is the top of the hill and takeoff point for hikers. Some room for parking. Keep straight ahead.

Mile 11.2 — Pass 50 spur.

Mile 12.4— Pass 60 spur on right leads down hill about a mile to parking area and another half mile to Cokely Bowl ski development. Keep left for St. Mary's Lake.

Mile 13.9 — Spur road on right leads to St. Mary's Lake. We drove another mile beyond the lake for more views, but this part of drive is mostly through rather ugly slash, although there is a little forestland.

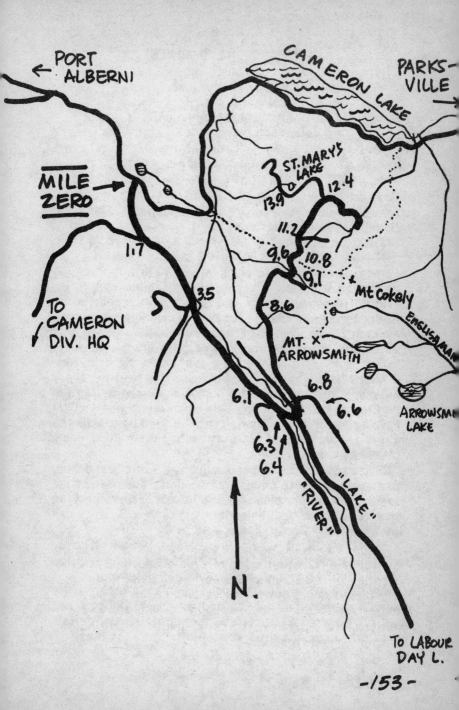

PORT
ALBERNI ←

CAMERON LAKE

PARKS-
VILLE →

ST. MARYS
LAKE

12.4

13.9

MILE
ZERO →

11.2

9.6   10.8

9.1

1.7

8.6

Mt Cokely

ENGLISHMAN

3.5

TO
CAMERON
DIV. HQ
↓

MT. X
ARROWSMITH

6.8

6.1

6.6 →

ARROWSMITH
LAKE

6.3
6.4

"RIVER"

"LAKE"

N.
↑

TO LABOUR
DAY L.

-153-

NANAIMO LAKES ROAD
TO STEELHEAD POOLS

Nanaimo River offers some fine steelheading and 13 miles along the Nanaimo River road brings you to the Crown Zellerbach gate, entrance to a network of trout fishing lakes and to the Green Mountain skiing slopes.

The Crown Zellerbach network of logging roads goes all the way through to connect up with the CZ Nitinat camp and the Cowichan Lake - Nitinat network of roads.

The Nanaimo River can be approached from logging roads on the south bank or from the Nanaimo Lakes - Green Mountain road on the north. Our trip will be along the north bank to the lakes country.

Cross the Nanaimo River bridge at Cassidy. You can start your fishing right below the bridge.

Turn left at the first turning, about 100 yards after the bridge and keep left.

Almost as soon as as you can get around the bend in the road you will see trails and rough roads leading off towards the river. They all lead to fishing spots.

Pass through a Boy Scout tree farm area for a short distance and just before a big gravel pit on the right, turn left down a bumpy road. Drive along this road for about half a mile to a parking spot on the right, just before the road heads down a bumpy hill, which could give trouble driving back up if you were to continue on. Best to walk the rest of the way. About 100 yards along the road, or trail, forks. Keep right.

If you keep left you come to some high bluffs overlooking deep still pools with a high rock wall on either side of the river. It is not easy climbing down the mossbank cliffs to the river 60 or 70 feet below, but you can get down to fish the pools.

For our trip, walk another couple of hundred yards on the trail and come to the top of a hill overlooking a lovely river pool. It is a steep incline at first on loose gravel and said, then it slopes out to a moss-covered hill for 50 yards to the river. This is a pool, about 50 yards long and 25 yards wide, shallow on the north bank, gently sloping out to become very deep and still.

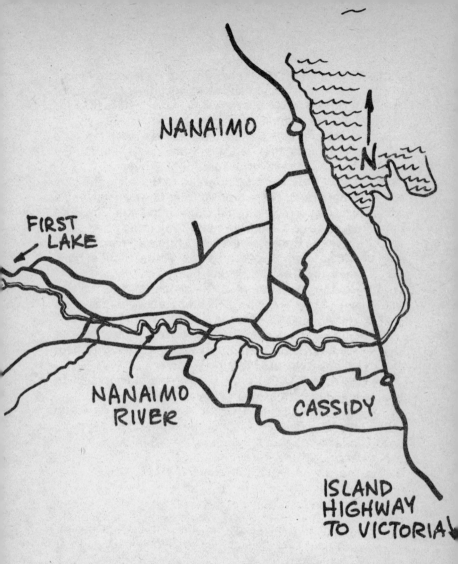

NANAIMO

FIRST LAKE

NANAIMO RIVER

CASSIDY

N

ISLAND HIGHWAY TO VICTORIA

At the top end there is a pot-holed narrow gore, through which the river empties into the pool, At the lower end there is a canyon and plenty of white water. The steelhead fight their way up the rapids and then rest in the pool, along the wall on the south side.

Back at your parked car look for a foot trail leading upstream on the left. It leads to a steep gorge between the hole just visited and the Bore Hole upstream. It is all fast water with rock wall on either side, but a steep trail leads to the water and you can fish the back eddies. At one point you can't climb around the rock wall and you have to crawl through a small tunnel.

Back to the mainline Nanaimo Lakes road, keep left for a few hundred yards, then left along the power line for the Bore Hole, one of the favorite spots on the river.

You can see the river far below and to the left is the long and wide Bore Hole. There are two trails down and on one a ladder has been provided to climb down the wall. The Bore Hole can also be reached from south bank trails.

Just above the Bore Hole is some white water where fish may be taken, and then comes the White Rapids Hole, which was known as the jigging hole.

Back to the mainline road, keep left to the railway trestle and see lovely pools below and above it. Carry on further and you find other roads leading to the river.

A few miles upstream is fast water where special techniques and 20 to 30-pound test line are used to haul the steelhead from the turbulent water.

The Nanaimo River in recent years has been closed to angling for salmon from May 1 to Sept. 30.

Taffy Merriman and Tony Turner caught these fish in Panther Lake, behind the Crown Zellerbach gates near Nanaimo.

SYSTEM OF TROUT-FILLED LAKES
BEHIND CROWN ZELLERBACH GATE

About six miles along the Nanaimo Lakes road from the Nanaimo River bridge turnoff at Cassidy you come to an intersection on the right, which is the lakes road cutoff.

Along this road it is 2.6 miles to intersection with Harewood Road. Left goes to Old Lakes Road, Crystal Lake and Ski Hill. Turn right for alternate route to Nanaimo and 2.3 miles along you come to Nanaimo Fish and Game Club complex entrance.

About 12 miles along the Nanaimo Lakes mainline road you come to the old Deadwood grade on the right. We have driven along this grade to Blackjack - Boomerang Lake chain and on to Northwest Bay, but that was some years ago and it was in rough shape then. I doubt it is passable now. Probably the bridge over the north fork of Nanaimo River (Deadwood Creek) is out now. But at times there is good winter steelheading in that creek.

Rainbows and cutthroats abound in the several lakes behind the Crown Zellerbach gate, which is 13 miles along the Nanaimo Lakes road, from the Nanaimo bridge at Cassidy.

But, before you go through the gate turn left down a gravel road, sometimes a little rough, leading about half a mile to the lower end of two-mile-long First Lake. This is a 24-hour access road for fishermen and is excellent for small boat access. CZ has provided a campsite here and at other lakes within its Nanaimo Lake logging claim, where weekend overnight stays are now permitted and no permits are now required.

Sometimes in early spring the cutthroats drop down from the Nanaimo River and there is excellent fishing in the narrow part of First Lake opposite the access area.

At this access spot you will see some of about 57 squatter cabins, which were established before the days of logging and have been passed down from father to son.

A string of logs across First Lake often prevents boat access up to the top end of the lake where in the spring there is some hot fly fishing in the short stretch of the Nanaimo River which separates First and Second Lakes.

But, you can go through the gate during open hours and drive four miles to the CZ camp and put your boat in there, or better still you can drive a couple of hundred yards past the camp, take the first turn left, cross the bridge over the Nanaimo River and find easy cartop launching on the left and some of the fishiest-looking water you could hope to find.

One mile past the camp you get your first glimpse of Second Lake, beautiful, but not the best for fishing.

There is another gate at Second Lake and fishermen could find it locked in the evenings after working hours, but open on weekends. The ski slopes of Green Mountain can be seen across the lake.

Cartop boats can be launched at the far end of the lake and also at the far end turn right for seven miles over fairly good gravel road for Panther and Echo Lakes.

Panther is a beautiful shallow lake, just the right size to fish from a rowboat. Generally it produces bigger trout than Echo and we have found a Tom Thumb fly works well.

But at the far end of Second Lake you should keep straight ahead for Third and Fourth Lakes and scores of fishy looking, but little fished spots along the Nanaimo River.

Third Lake is seven miles from the camp and not much more than a mud pond.

Ten Miles from the camp turn left for Green Mountain skiing grounds.

Twelve miles from the camp, turn left for a short gravel road to Fourth Lake and some pretty fair fishing.

Straight ahead would lead to the Nitinat gate, and just before that gate a right turn leads to BCFP claims and Tuck Lake trout fishing. But at the time of writing the road beyond Fourth Lake was not open as a recreational access road.

There are some other fishing lakes in the area, but they mostly require a bit of hiking ... Labor Day, Heart, Williams and Moriarity are some of the better known among the smaller lakes.

MAPS ON FOLLOWING PAGES..

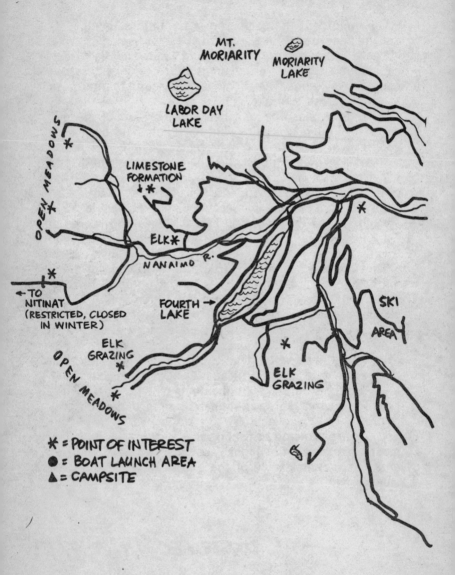

MT.
MORIARITY

MORIARITY
LAKE

LABOR DAY
LAKE

OPEN MEADOWS

LIMESTONE
FORMATION
*

ELK *

NANAIMO R.

*

←TO
NITINAT
(RESTRICTED, CLOSED
IN WINTER)

FOURTH
LAKE →

ELK
GRAZING
*

OPEN MEADOWS

*

ELK
GRAZING

SKI

AREA

* = POINT OF INTEREST
● = BOAT LAUNCH AREA
▲ = CAMPSITE

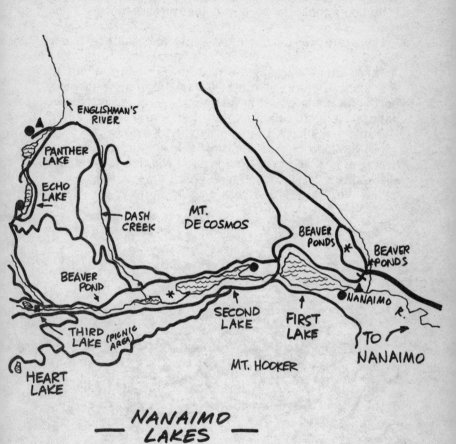

ENGLISHMAN'S
RIVER

PANTHER
LAKE

ECHO
LAKE

DASH
CREEK

MT.
DE COSMOS

BEAVER
PONDS

BEAVER
PONDS

BEAVER
POND

NANAIMO R.

NANAIMO

SECOND
LAKE

FIRST
LAKE

TO
NANAIMO

THIRD
LAKE (PICNIC
AREA)

HEART
LAKE

MT. HOOKER

— NANAIMO —
LAKES —

TWO ACCESS ROUTES LEAD
TO LAKES BACK OF NANAIMO

North of Nanaimo and back on the ridges to the west is some fine hunting and fishing country with a chain of eight little lakes that can be conveniently reached by logging roads.

There are two main access points to these fish happy lakes.

There are no logging gates to stop you when you turn off the Island Highway at the Somerset Hotel at Wellington, north of Nanaimo, but the road this way can be just about impassable in the early part of the season, especially if logging trucks have been working in the area.

You can follow MacMillan Bloedel mainline roads to this fishing area at all hours now and you will find them in fair shape. MB's Northwest Bay Division map is the one to follow. We will describe both access routes.

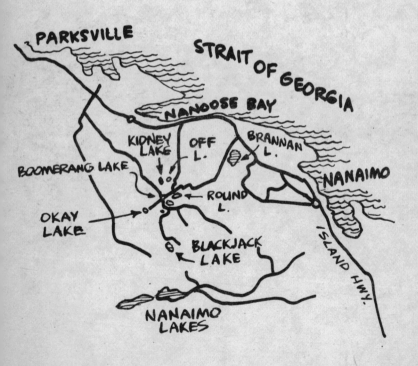

BLACKJACK ALWAYS OPEN
BUT CAN BE ROUGH

For the more difficult, but always open entry, leave the Island Highway north of Nanaimo, on to the old Island Highway at Somerset Hotel. Half a mile along turn left at the Pleasant Valley hall on to Blackjack Road.

Call that turn Mile Zero.

Mile 2.5— First sight of Brannan Lake. Take the first left fork for public access. There are rainbow trout, cutthroat and kokanee in Brannan Lake.

Mile 6.5 miles— Turner Road junction. Left goes to main line logging road and to Boomerang, Cottle, Okay Lakes. Right goes to Round, Off and Kidney Lakes. We go right first.

Mile 6.9 —'T' in road. One-quarter mile to right is Round Lake, a small pond, but sometimes teeming with rainbows up to five pounds. Several paths lead to lake.

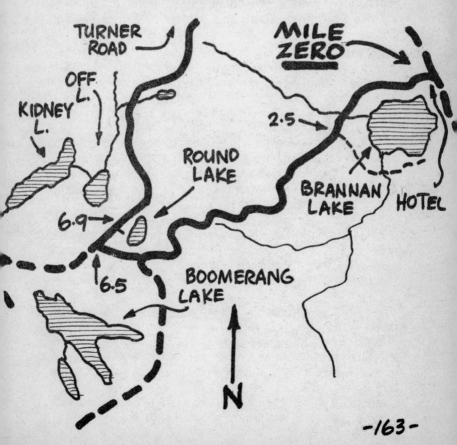

Mile 8.7 — Off Lake, another small lake, but loaded with rainbows. From Off Lake you can walk to Kidney Lake, or if you carried on 4 1/2 miles you would reach Nanoose.

Mile 10.6 — Back to T in road, and keep straight ahead.

Mile 12.3 — Y in road. Take either way and 50 feet along leads to junction with mainline logging road. Note this point for future reference on the other access roads. Approaching junction this way, right goes 8.8 miles to Northwest Bay. Left goes to Boomerang, Cottle, Blackjack Lakes and Benson and Wolfe Mountain hunting areas. Straight ahead across junction goes to Okay Lake, which is where we go for side trip.

Mile 14.5 — Okay Lake, good fly fishing in spring for Kamloops trout, and surrounding country good for deer and grouse hunting.

Mile 16.5 — Back at intersection. Turn right.

Mile 17.2 — First access to Boomerang Lake, which was rehabilitated by fish and wildlife branch in October, 1958, stocked with rainbows in fall of 1959 (and had fish plantings several times since) and opened to fishing in June, 1960.

Mile 17.6 — Second access to Boomerang Lake, and an intersection on right leading to Cottle Lake and Blackjack Lake. Boat float and nice camping and picnicking spot on Boomerang. In story about second access note way to reach far side of the lake, from the 12.3 -mile Y intersection.

Carry on three miles for some of the best shooting ground in the Nanaimo district. Half a mile along a right turn leads to Blackjack Mountain hunting area between Mount Benson and Siwash Ridges. Numerous side logging spurs lead to hunting areas.

Mile 23.5 — Back at Boomerang Lake and turn left for Cottle (or Chain) Lake, 100 yards up the road. Cottle was rehabilitated same time as Boomerang. You can launch cartop boat from road.

Mile 24 — Blackjack Farm pond below. No fish report on it.

Mile 24.7 — Y in road, keep left and then at next Y, keep right.

Mile 25.6 — See Deadwood Creek Valley ahead, Blackjack Mountain on left and Amor de Cosmos Mountain, right front. This is rough, overgrown road, but you can get through.

Mile 27.1 — Another Y in road. Keep left for Blackjack Lake, 200 yards along, where you can launch a car-topper.

There are natural spawn cutthroat trout in Blackjack, to the point of being over-crowded with trout.

We have gone through from here to the Nanaimo Lakes Road (as described in that chapter) but it probably is not possible to make it now. Anyway here is the mileage at that time.

Mile 27.5 — Back on road in Anderson Creek draw between Blackjack and Wolfe for good hunting, but rough going.

Mile 29.5 — Turn right up a short, rough hill and left on to better road.

Mile 30.6 — Bridge over north fork of Nanaimo River (Deadwood Creek) where there is good trout fishing at times and steelhead in winter months. This bridge is probably washed out.

Mile 30.7 — On to Comox Logging Deadwood grade and into elk country.

Mile 32.2 — On to Nanaimo Lakes Road, about one mile from CZ gate.

I would suggest any adventuresome travellers wanting to explore this Anderson Creek draw - Deadwood region should approach it from the Nanaimo Lakes road.

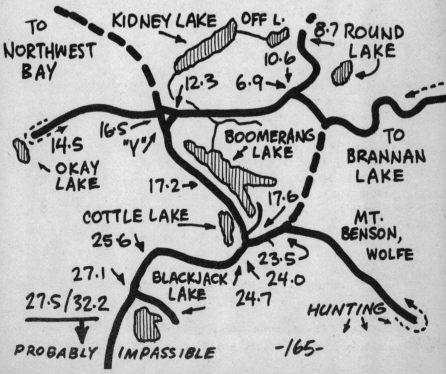

Boomerang Lake, reached best from MB's Northwest Bay roads, provides camping, boating and trout fishing.

Scenic spots reached by logging roads from Great Central Lake is the Ash River flowing from Dixon Lake.

John Ebert plays steelhead in Oyster River.

NORTHWEST BAY ACCESS
EASIEST TO BOOMERANG

To take the easier route to Boomerang and the other lakes, carry on along the Island Highway to the Northwest Bay MB logging camp, which is south of Parksville where the yellow light flashes.

Turn left and drive through the logging camp.

Mile Zero — Logging gate. Keep on mainline.

Mile .9 — Intersection, keep left. Straight ahead are miles of logging roads to explore, leading to headwaters of Englishman River.

Mile 3.2 — Intersection, keep left.

Mile 3.7 — Intersection, keep left.

Mile 8.8 — Intersection and Y. This is the Mile 12.3 mark in the Turner Road access described earlier.

Left on the Y would go to the alternative Turner Road route, but also goes to the north arm of Boomerang, which we mentioned earlier, and will describe later; and to Round, Off and Kidney Lakes. Right goes the 2.2 miles to Okay Lake described earlier. Continue straight ahead on mainline for Boomerang Lake.

Mile 9.4 — First access to Boomerang. Room for one camper.

Mile 9.8 — Second access to Boomerang. Room for three or four self-contained campers and boat launching.

Back to the Y intersection. Mile 8.8 in this access and Mile 12.3 in the Turner Road access.

Turn right on to the Turner Road route and drive just .6 miles for a right turn on road, hardly more than a trail.

Some distance along — it seems long because it is rough driving — you come to an intersection. You can turn right and less than a quarter of a mile along you come to a parking area within sight of the lake. A lakeshore trail leads to a path along the north shore of Boomerang Lake.

At the intersection you could drive a quarter of a mile further along, swinging to the right, and reach the lake at a raft where you could launch a boat. But we walked back along that road and no way would we have tried to drive it. Better reconoitre first.

If you don't have a boat, the north arm of Boomerang is the spot for you. It has a very pleasant and sheltered shoreline with plenty of places to fish from shore. But if you do have a boat, put it in at the launching spot on the south shore and row around for a picnic on the north shore.

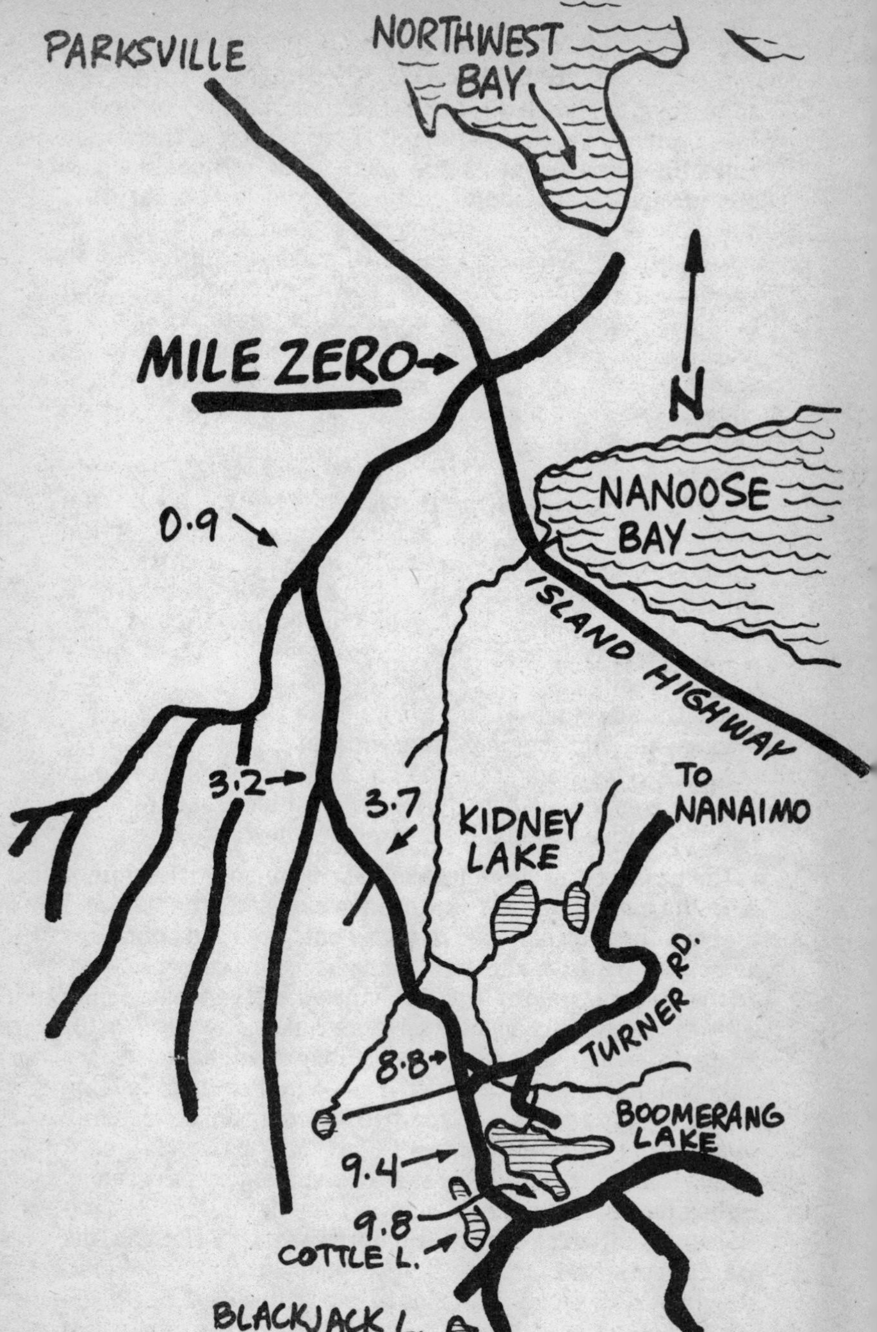

PARKSVILLE

NORTHWEST BAY

MILE ZERO→

N

NANOOSE BAY

0.9 ↘

ISLAND HIGHWAY

3.2→

3.7 ↙

KIDNEY LAKE

TO NANAIMO

TURNER RD.

8.8→

BOOMERANG LAKE

9.4→

9.8 ↙

COTTLE L.

BLACKJACK L.

SPIDER LAKE FOR BASS
HORNE LAKE FOR TROUT

Spider Lake gives up heavier small-mouth bass than any other Vancouver Island Lake and Horne Lake can provide four to six-pound cutthroat trout in February and March when the frost is still on the ground.

And the Big Qualicum River which flows out of Horne Lake is a temperature and flow-controlled river that provides some good winter steelheading water. It also is a federal fisheries maternity river and visitors should be sure to take in the counting fence, spawning and rearing channels, rearing ponds, marking lab and hatchery which are open to visitors.

To reach the Spider - Horne Lake area you turn left off the Island Highway at the Horne Lake garage, less than a mile before the Big Qualicum River. If you continue on the highway a few hundred yards, you will see the entrance to the Big Qualicum fisheries flow and temperature controlled river project and your inspection trip to that complex starts at the office buildings less than half a mile up that road.

But we now turn at the Horne Lake Garage. You drive through the old logging camp village.

Just .9 miles along from the highway turnoff you come to the intersection of the Horne Lake public road (on the right) and the logging road straight ahead.

The best way for Spider Lake bass fishing in the summer is up the logging road. You will pass alongside the lake and that is where you can launch your boat. The road continues on to join up with the public road.

It is 3.9 miles along the public road to the intersection with the logging road along Horne Lake.

But from that first stretch of public road, a little more than two miles along, the third turn on the left after leaving the village, is the access road to the Illusion Lakes, and, eventually to Spider Lake.

This is a short road, almost a trail, coming to a dead-end, with room for a couple of campers, alongside the second Illusion Lake, which isn't much more than a big slough. This area is now park reserve.

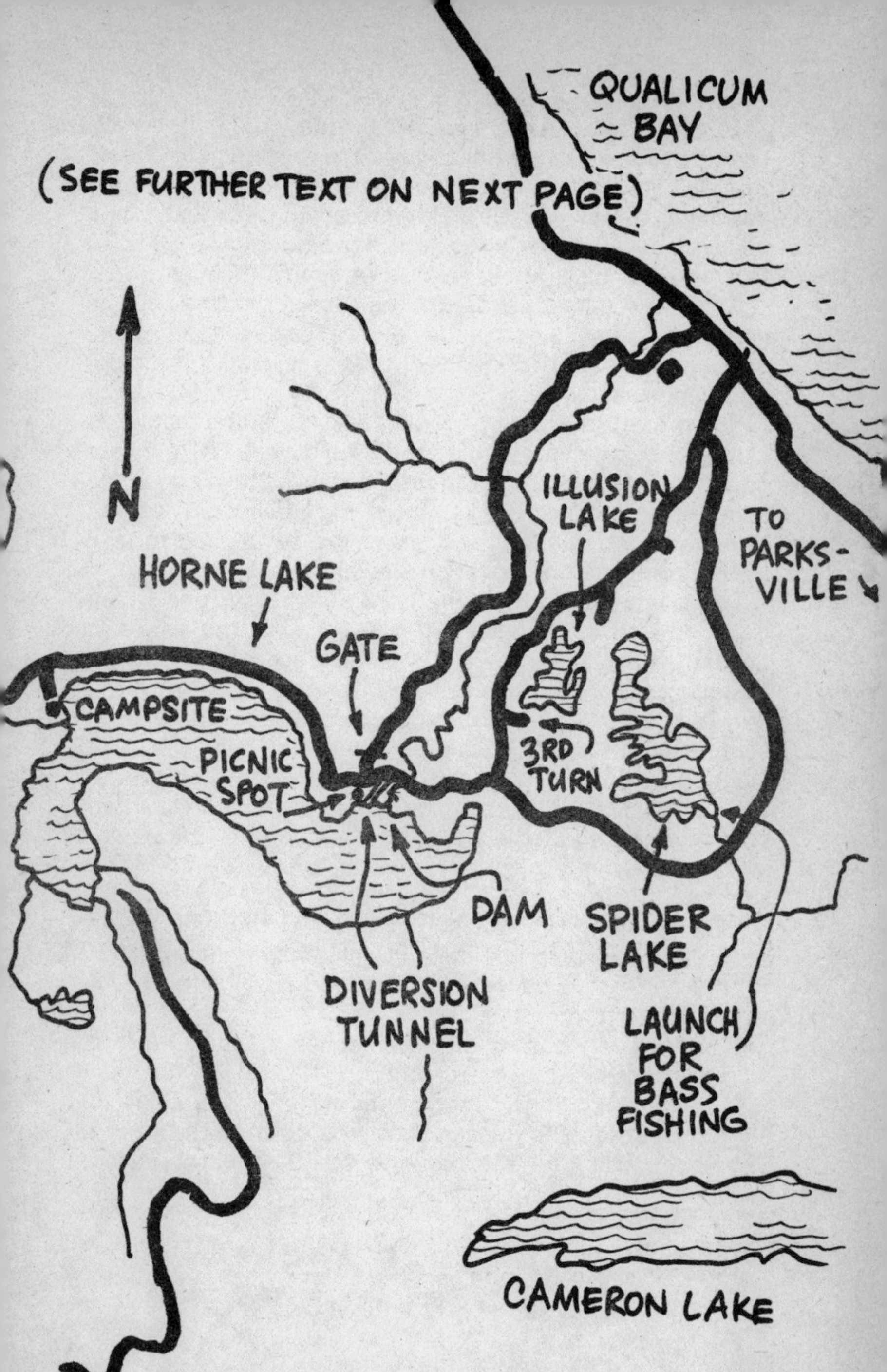

QUALICUM BAY

(SEE FURTHER TEXT ON NEXT PAGE)

N

ILLUSION LAKE

TO PARKS-VILLE

HORNE LAKE

GATE

CAMPSITE

PICNIC SPOT

3RD TURN

DAM

SPIDER LAKE

DIVERSION TUNNEL

LAUNCH FOR BASS FISHING

CAMERON LAKE

To get to Spider Lake from here is fairly difficult, but we have done it when we have found the logging gate closed.

It isn't difficult to launch in the Illusion Lake, but then you have to row across the lake, about 200 feet. Then follows a portage over a rough trail to Spider Lake, 50 to 75 feet straight up a knoll, and down again.

Going down the other side of the knoll is almost as bad as going up, because you have to hold back on your boat. There is only about 150 feet between lakes, but it is almost straight up and down.

Now we return to the public-logging road intersection at Horne Lake at the 3.9-mile mark. Turn right for the west end of Horne Lake and 1.4 miles along is the turning for the fisheries dam which blocks off the Big Qualicum River, so the new fisheries intake and tunnel can be utilized to take water from three temperature levels of the lake.

There is a little picnicking area at the dam and if you carry on and keep right you will come to the fisheries department gate which stops vehicle access to the Big Qualicum River. But you can park your car there and it is only a half-mile walk until you come to the upper-river steelheading waters of the Big Qualicum. You can hike along the road and riverbanks for six miles downstream to the mouth of the Big Qualicum. It is a good idea to use two cars, one parked at the upper gate and one at the downstream fisheries project parking lot, to provide a shuttle service.

To drive along Horne Lake keep left at the dam picnic area and it can be a terrible, pot-holed nightmarish drive, but not dangerous because the roadbed is solid, for 5 1/2 miles along Horne Lake.

About 5.3 miles from the intersection (at the 3.9-mile mark) you come to a power line.

At the power line the road continues until you come to Big Horne Creek and you can then walk down to the mouth where you will find the bar and the best early-season fishing.

(SEE MAP OF THESE AREAS
ON PREVIOUS PAGE)

This logging road does continue on beyond Big Horne Creek and comes out north of Qualicum Bay in the vicinity of Rosewall Creek. And you can even take another turn on the left and take this logging road all the way to the Cherry Creek Road in the Albernis.

But sometimes that road is impassable and always it is rugged. There is a steep hill with loose stone on the way from Horne Lake to the Albernis and it is next to impossible to climb that hill with anything but a four-wheel drive. It is a little easier to drive from the Albernis to Horne Lake, because that way you drive down that terrible hill.

You can camp at the parking area by the Big Horne Creek. There is a delightful camping area along the lakeshore, reached by turning left between the power line and the Big Horne Creek. The road is obvious, narrow, a little scary at times as you nearly teeter into the lake, but you end up at a lovely camping and picnicking area. Both camping areas make ideal bases for hikers wishing to explore the Horne Lake caves.

COURTENAY PLAYGROUND
SHOWN IN NEW CZ MAP

Crown Zellerbach has published a new series of recreational guide maps for 11 of its British Columbia logging divisions and five of them are about Vancouver Island.

CZ has had recreational maps for some of its logging divisions for several years, but they had rather sketchy information. The new maps are far more interesting and reflect CZ's new policy of providing better access and camping, picnicking and boat launching facilities for visitors.

Divisions covered on Vancouver Island include Nitinat, Ladysmith's Nanaimo Lakes, Courtenay, Beaver Cove and Johnstone Straits.

The Courtenay division roads lead to exciting playgrounds for fishermen, hunters, skiers, mountain climbers, summer hikers and boaters.

This division may be entered from the Lake Trail Road near Cumberland, or from MB's Iron River road at Oyster Bay, where the CZ road connects a short distance after entering the logging road from the Island Highway.

Kinsmen Club has provided a campground and boat launching on Comox Lake and nearby at the start of its Comox logging road system CZ has also provided a boat launch.

One CZ mainline follows the entire length of Comox Lake, leading to trails to the Comox Glacier.

This same road makes a right turn on the South Main Road, along the Cruikshanks River to trails that lead to alpine Moat Lake, Circlet Lake, beautiful Paradise Meadows and Forbidden Plateau hiking areas and summer fishing lakes.

The Royston-Duncan Bay Main Line leads from the Cumberland CZ headquarters, alongside Wolf Lake, across and alongside Tsolum River, Oyster River and Quinsam River, all the way to Duncan Bay pulp mill, north of Campbell River.

In the Beaver Cove division (which is covered more fully in the second volume of Logging Road Travels, Campbell River to Cape Scott) CZ has provided a camping area and boat launch at the southern tip of Bonanza Lake, a picnic site at the north end of Bonanza Lake, and a boat launch at Ida Lake.

This has been the main North Island Road, but the new government road alongside Nimpkish Lake to Woss, and eventually through the Schoen-Tsitika to Kelsey Bay, will mean the Bonanza Lake road will revert to a logging-recreational access road.

The Johnstone Strait map mainly shows a CZ logging road on Quadra Island, with a camping and picnic site adjacent to the marine park near Hoskyn Channel.

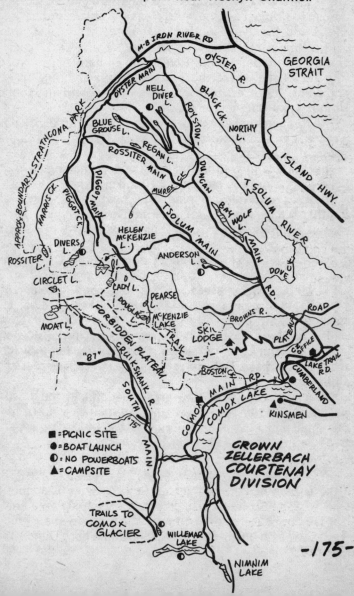

CIRCLE TRIP
...COWICHAN TO NANAIMO

The new CZ maps for Nitinat and Ladysmith division show the connecting road between the two divisions. This road is impassable during the winter, but it means that in spring-summer-fall conditions (except when there is extreme fire hazard) recreationists will be able to make a circle trip via Cowichan Lake, through the Nitinat division across the ridge road, down to Nanaimo Lakes and back to the Island Highway, south of Nanaimo.

The Nitinat recreational map shows the new CZ campsite on the upper Nitinat River, the 24-hour access road into Tuck Lake where there is wilderness camping areas, and points travellers to the Nanaimo Lakes, and also to the Nitinat Lake-Bamfield area.

The Nanaimo Lakes area within the Ladysmith division is a recreationist's paradise and the new CZ map shows the points of interest.

There is a campground and small boat launching on First Lake, just before you enter the CZ road system.

There is another camping and boat launch spot at Panther Lake, where we have found some good early season fishing with a Tom Thumb fly. There is a boat launching spot on adjacent Echo Lake.

A 24-hour access road before entering the CZ system leads along Deadwood Creek to beaver ponds.

Elk winter grazing areas are beside Second Lake and at several other points in the Nanaimo Lakes area — all marked on the map.

Fish and wildlife branch has reserved Third Lake for kid's only fishing, 15 and under. CZ has provided a picnic area at Third Lake. Between second and third lake there is a beaver pond.

You can drive up to the open meadows at the headwaters of the Nanaimo River and the mainline skirts the Nanaimo River for several miles. Several other open meadow areas are shown on the map.

A trail leads from the end of the roads to Labor Day Lake.

The Green Mountain skiing area is reached by a road in this CZ vacationland.

Those are the Vancouver Island CZ maps available, but if you are planning a holiday elsewhere in B.C., CZ has maps of its Bella Coola area, Kitimat, Kelowna, Armstrong, Lumbs divisions and its Sandspit operations on the Queen Charlottes.

If you wish to obtain any of these maps you may write to Crown Zellerbach, Public Relations Department, 1030 West Georgia Street, Vancouver, B.C.

SEE OYSTER RIVER
FROM LOGGING ROADS

Logging roads from Oyster Bay and Campbell River take you to explore the middle reaches of the Oyster River.

Easiest access is by MB's Iron River Road, first turn on the left after passing the provincial picnic site at Oyster Bay.

From that turn it is 3.1 miles up the Iron River road to a left turn which cuts back towards the river. From there the road is really just an overgrown trail and willows and small firs slap against your vehicle. You might even have to use a trail bike, four-wheel drive vehicle for the less than one mile to the river.

Just .7 miles along that overgrown road-trail you come out into the Oyster River flats at a junction.

A sharp right turn for .3 miles takes you to an upstream river spot with a picnic site on a sandy pool, a little falls and some nice fishing water.

From this junction you can also park and walk straight ahead through a young pine forest to the river where you can fish and follow the river path upstream or downstream.

You can also keep left and straight ahead at the junction and drive 1.6 to a turn-around where another trail leads to the river, and another .6 miles leads to the broken bridge over the Little Oyster. A road from the highway reaches this bridge, but you can't cross.

You can park at this bridge and follow the trail for 200 yards down the Little Oyster to the junction with the Big Oyster where there is big fishing water, including a fishy looking riffle. With chest waders you could even walk and wade back and forth until you reach the main highway bridge.

Back on the Iron River road intersection at the 3.1-mile mark, you can turn left and carry on up the road.

You pass under the power line after 1.3 miles along this road and on the left is a fine view of the Oyster River winding far below and the Forbidden Plateau in the distance.

Another 1.9 miles through forest plantation and you come to a junction with Comox Logging Road, and a right turn will take you 13 miles, sometimes along the Quinsam River, to the junction near the Campbell River bridge.

But instead of turning right, keep straight ahead at the junction for .3 miles to another junction and again keep left for another .3 miles for the bridge over the Oyster and a spectacular view of the Oyster River Canyon.

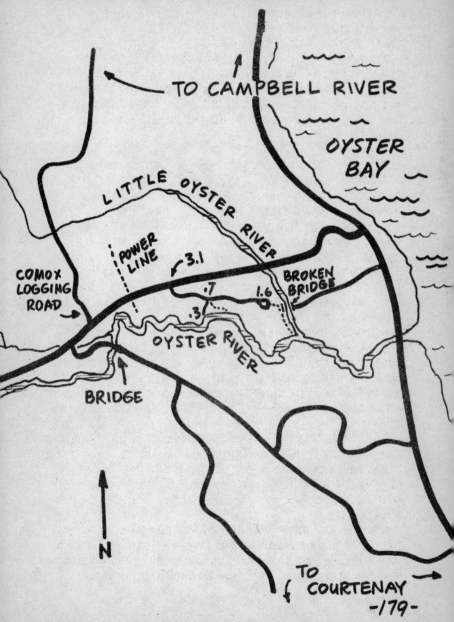

TO CAMPBELL RIVER

OYSTER BAY

LITTLE OYSTER RIVER

POWER LINE

COMOX LOGGING ROAD

3.1

.7

.3

1.6

BROKEN BRIDGE

OYSTER RIVER

BRIDGE

N

TO COURTENAY

Forbidden Plateau Lodge.

Logging roads climb to base of Mount Arrowsmith for skiing, hiking and fishing.

MAPS

If you plan to have fun on Vancouver Island's logging roads you should make sure you are well equipped with maps.

First of all in your car or camper glove compartment you should have both these Saltaire **Logging Road Travel Guides— Victoria to Campbell River** and **Campbell River to Cape Scott**,which will give you as complete a description of Vancouver Island travel as you will find anywhere.

The provincial department of lands and forests and resources department, surveys and mapping branch, puts out several maps of Vancouver Island which may be obtained at nominal costs. Most useful is the SGS 1 map of the whole Island, showing all the main logging roads.

There are other larger scale maps available for different sections of the Island, as well as a handy folded Northern Vancouver Island map, which may be obtained free from tourist literature outlets.

All the major logging companies now supply a number of maps of their various logging claims and these may be obtained directly from the company headquarters, the division offices, and sometimes from sporting goods stores and tourist outlets in the various areas.

Doris Stastny also puts out excellent recreational maps of Campbell River and Buttle Lake, Northern Vancouver Island, and Courtenay and Buttle Lake areas, which may be purchased at various outlets in the areas they cover.

A WORD OF CAUTION ....

Although the logging roads described in this book are useable by "family cars", they are not paved, four-lane highways. In most instances the roads are gravel, sometimes dirt, wide enough for oncoming cars to pass with room to spare. However, they do narrow to one-lane width occasionally, and fallen rocks and potholes can sneak up on the unwary driver.

And although the restrictions, which usually allow public travel only during non-operating hours, make the roads ideal for "Sunday Drives" — a few simple precautions are in order.

—Make sure your car is in good operating condition.
—Carry a spare tire and changing equipment. (A container for carrying water is a good idea, too.)
—Have adequate gasoline for your trip.

One reason for the logging roads' appeal is their **ISOLATION AND LACK OF "CIVILIZATION"** — but this means gas stations and repair facilities are few and far between. And the B.C. Auto Association's rules say they will not provide road service . . . "When the vehicle has been driven into an area which is not a regularly travelled road (i.e. beaches, fields, creek beds, **logging or forest service roads** or other inaccessible areas)." (Emphasis ours.)

ABOUT THE AUTHORS

Alec Merriman is outdoors editor of The Daily Colonist in Victoria, B.C., and covers all fishing, hunting and general outdoor activities. In three columns a week he tells where the fish are and how to catch them, and how to have outdoors fun on Vancouver Island.

His first book, *Outdoors With Alec Merriman,* was a comprehensive guide to all Vancouver Island fishing, complete with maps and mile-by-mile directions to find the fishing spots, as well as a month-by-month calendar of the times and places to fish.

That book, first published in 1967, was a Canadian regional best seller and after three editions, has been completely revised with an outdoors calendar and special emphasis on freshwater fishing on Vancouver Island.

This book contains some of the trips described in that first book. The revised edition will be specially designed as companion for this book about logging road travel. This book is also a companion book for his second book, *How To Catch Steelhead,* now in its second revised edition, and *Salmon*

Fishing With The Experts.

Since he left the Colonist's political beat in 1960 to take up outdoor writing Alec and his wife, Taffy, a war bride from Wales, have been deeply involved in the opening up of the logging roads on Vancouver Island for recreational use.

There was no general public access to logging areas when they first took to the outdoors full time in 1960.

Since then the opening of the logging roads for recreationists has been one of their major objectives.

This book is a monument to their success. Wife Taffy, as Alec describes his war bride, has been a constant companion and helpmate on all their outdoor trips.

As logging roads were opened for public access they were always among the first to travel on them and to record their amenities for public recreation.

So extensive have been their logging road travels that it has taken two books to describe them — one covering the roads from *Victoria* to *Campbell River* and the other from *Campbell River* to *Cape Scott.*

For more than a decade they have acted as a liaison between logging company operators and recreationists. They have blasted recreationists who have vandalized and stolen logging company properties. And they have lambasted logging companies when they have been reticent about public access. They have been relentless in their campaign for better logging practices to preserve the environment for all users.

But, always they have tried to be fair to all users of the forestlands.

They believe the use of the forests can be shared by all users . . . and that is what this book is about . . . the integrated use of the people's forest lands for the benefit of all users . . . fish, game, consumers and recreationists.

YOU WILL ALSO ENJOY SALTAIRE'S OTHER 'HOW-TO' BOOKS

How to Catch Salmon!

by Charles White

Now in its fifth printing, this information-packed book is one of our most popular! Contains basic information on Trolling patterns; How to rig tackle; Fisheries Department information on most productive lures; Proper depths to fish; Salmon habit patterns; How to play and net your fish; Where to **find** fish! Full of diagrams and illustrations! **How to Catch Salmon** is **the** basic book on salmon fishing in the North Pacific!
Revised Edition
$1.50

How to Catch Salmon - Advanced Techniques!

The most comprehensive salmon fishing book available! Over 250 pages, crammed full of how-to tips and easy-to-follow diagrams! Covers **all** popular salmon fishing methods: **Downrigger** Techniques; Mooching; Trolling with bait; Tricks with Spoons and Plugs; Tips for river mouth fishing; Catching giant Tyees; Winter Fishing; Secrets of Dodger & Flasher fishing; Buzz bombs, Deadly Dicks, Sneaks and other casting lures -
AND MUCH MORE!
$3.95

Bucktails and Hoochies!
by Bruce Colegrave & Jack Gaunt

Trolling bucktail flies is the most exciting method of catching salmon — and very productive using the methods described by bucktail expert Bruce Colegrave. Hoochies have always been the favorite of commercial fishermen and are catching on rapidly with sportsmen. Commercial expert Jack Gaunt provides a special section on how-to catch salmon with hoochies.
$1.95

Salmon Fishing with the Experts!

Well known outdoors writer Alec Merriman explains in detail the fishing methods of the **top salmon experts** on Vancouver Island! Includes how to fish Campbell River, Saanich Inlet, Pedder-Becher Bay, Alberni Canal and other West Coast hot spots! Covers trolling, mooching, buzz bombs, bucktail flies!

Hundreds of photos and diagrams.
$2.95

How to Catch Trout!

by Lee Straight

Lee Straight has been fish & game columnist for the Vancouver Sun for more than 28 years. Regarded as one of western Canada's top outdoorsmen. **How to Catch Trout** contains many fish catching "secrets" from his own wide experience and from the experts with whom he has fished! The book contains chapters on Trolling, Still Fishing, Best Equipment, Casting, Ice Fishing, Best Baits and Lures, River and Lake fishing methods - and much more! Diagrams and illustrations by Nelson Dewey.
$1.95

How to Catch Bottomfish!

While salmon are the "Glamor" fish, **bottomfish** are everyday **Good Eating** - and easy to catch! This book shows how to catch Cod, Sole, Perch, Snapper, Rockfish, and other tasty bottomfish. Tells best tackle & rigs; baits; when and where to fish! Covers Drift-fishing, Trolling, Casting from shore. Plus easy-to-make "Super Lure"! Detailed step-by-step filleting diagrams!

**Revised and Expanded
$1.95**

How to Catch Crabs!

Now in a fifth printing, with revisions that show latest crabbing techniques! Tells how to catch crabs with traps, scoops, rings! **Where, when** and **how** to set traps! Best baits! Detailed description and illustrations of a much **easier** method of cleaning, cooking and shelling the meat! A great book, crammed-full of all you need to know about **How to Catch Crabs.**

Newly Expanded Edition! $1.50

How to Catch Shellfish!

How, when and where to find and catch many forms of tasty shellfish! **Oysters, Clams, Shrimp,** mussels, limpets. Easiest way to shuck oysters. Best equipment for clamming and shrimping! When **not** to eat certain shellfish! **What to eat** and **what to discard!** Easy ways to open and clean shellfish! How to outrace a razor clam. A delightful book chock-full of useful information! Illustrated.

Newly Expanded Edition! $1.95

How to Hunt Deer and Other Game!

by Lee Straight

Popular fish & game columnist Lee Straight does it again with this information-packed book on big (and smaller) game hunting in Northwestern U.S. and western Canada! Covers Deer, Elk, Moose, Bear, Wolf, Cougar and many more! Chapters on gun & ammo selection; proper gear; tracking; **still-hunting** and **"driving"** methods; field butchering game. Plus - special section on **where** and **when** to hunt!
$1.95

How to Catch Steelhead!

by Alec Merriman

Now in a third printing, this book by popular Outdoors columnist Alec Merriman contains much valuable information for either **novice or expert** steelheader! Tells how to "read" the water to find steelhead! Proper weight and bait hookups. Bottom-bouncing. How to preserve bait! Techniques for fishing either clear or murky water! Fly fish for Steelhead! Many diagrams and illustrations.
$1.95

How to Cook Your Catch!

by Jean Challenger

A "must have" companion for our "How-to-Catch books! Tells how to cook on board a boat, at a cabin or campsite! Shortcuts in preparing seafood for cooking! Cleaning and filleting! Recipes and methods for preparing delicious meals using simple camp utensils! Special section on exotic seafoods! Illustrated.
$1.95

Microwave Cooking

NEW FROM SALTAIRE!

An expert in the field reveals Microwave Cooking How-to, background, cooking tips and hints, converting your standard recipes to microwave, how to select an oven — and much more. Ideal for anyone. Contemplating owning microwave — perfect for those who already do! Plus! Many, many Recipes!

$2.95

Logging Road Travel

with Alec & Taffy Merriman

Over **TWO THOUSAND MILES** of private logging roads on Vancouver Island are now open to the general public! These graded roads into previously inaccessible wilderness areas can usually be explored in the family car or camper! Mile-by-mile guides show you through this backwoods wonderland! Exact mileages with detailed maps and directions make these books a vital part of any logging road outing!

Volume 1 - Victoria to Campbell River (Revised) $3.95

Volume 2 - Campbell River to Cape Scott $2.95 each

Outdoors with Alec Merriman!

A regional best seller! (Over 18,000 copies sold!) Features new **Outdoors Fun Calendar** telling how, when and where to enjoy the outdoors on Vancouver Island! Contains valuable data, expert tips on trout lies and steelhead runs. Stream by stream and pool by pool directions for best fishing spots. Expanded edition; new maps and illustrations; new fishing and hunting information! **$2.95**

Okanagan Back Roads
by Dave Stewart

Prince George Backroads
by Ken & Kathy Bernsohn

NOW PRINTING!

Using a format similar to our best-selling (Vancouver Island) "Logging Road Travel" books, freelance writer and outdoorsman Dave Stewart gives mile-by-mile coverage of Okanagan highways and byways. Detailed maps and directions make it easy to find your way to great picnicing, hiking, fishing, hunting, sightseeing, rock & gem collecting, etc.

Vol 1 -- South - Central Okanagan

Vol 2 -- North Okanagan Shuswap.
$3.95 each

Latest in our Logging Road/Back Road Series, outdoors writer Ken Bernsohn and wife Kathy travelled thousands of miles to find the most interesting Prince George area back-roads! Detailed maps and information to sightseeing, camping, hiking, rockhounding, exploring, fishing, hunting, picknicking!

$3.95

How to Escape the Rat Race!

by Charles White

Must reading for anyone who thinks his job or way of life has him trapped! Anyone can find himself in a rat race -- **executive, student, housewife -- even a retired person!**

How to Escape the Rat Race contains step-by-step information for the would-be "escapee", including Defining the Rat Race; Why You Feel You're In a Rat Race; Getting Rid of False Values; Finding the Kind of Life You Really Want; Finding the Money You Need . . . and much more! With cartoon illustrations by Nelson Dewey.
$1.25

How to Choose Your Booze!

How to get the best bargains in vodka and gin! **How to buy the best beer!** Full information on Whiskey, Liqueurs, Wines, Beers, Champagnes and much more! An extremely informative book -- and a necessity for anyone who buys alcoholic beverages. **Illustrated.**
$1.50

How to Win at the Stock Market!

by Art Phillips

Truly an expert on the stock market, Art Phillips gives concise details and reasoning behind investment methods and techniques! Charting; Statistics and their pitfalls; Earnings and their true value; Penny Stocks! **Valuable information** for **beginner** and **long-time** investor alike! Many charts and illustrations.
$2.00

50 Casseroles For Drunks!

NEW FROM SALTAIRE!

This shocking title introduces a very practical new cookbook. It contains recipes for 50 delicious casseroles with a special difference. They all have flexible cooking times, so you can leave them in the oven for an extra hour or so if your cocktail party runs over-time—hence the title!
128 pages, 4¼x7 inches.
.95

Take a Trip -- According to Doyle!

by Doyle Klyn

Cruise Ships... The Inside Story
by Gary Bannerman

NEW FROM SALTAIRE!

A seasoned world traveler and former columnist for **Weekend Magazine** ("According to Doyle"), Doyle Klyn writes with first-hand knowledge and insight. Packed with useful information, how-to-tips, traveller's "secrets", and delightful anecdotes, the book will be invaluable to anyone planning business or pleasure travel! Worthwhile, fun reading -- with cartoon illustrations by Nelson Dewey.
$1.50

Top investigative reporter Gary Bannerman reveals Behind-the-scenes, Below-decks, inside stories, anecdotes, tips, advice! Must reading if you're thinking of a cruise — Entertaining if you've already been!

$3.95

ORDER FORM

.... **HOW TO CATCH SALMON**
at $1.50 each .... $..........

.... **HOW TO CATCH SALMON -- ADVANCED TECHNIQUES**
at $3.95 each .... $..........

.... **WHERE TO FIND SALMON! -- Sooke to Cowichan Bay**
at $2.00 each .... $..........

.... **SALMON FISHING WITH THE EXPERTS!**
at $2.95 each .... $..........

.... **HOW TO COOK YOUR CATCH!**
at $1.95 each .... $..........

.... **HOW TO CATCH BOTTOMFISH!**
at $1.95 each .... $..........

.... **HOW TO CATCH CRABS!**
at $1.50 each .... $..........

.... **HOW TO CATCH SHELLFISH**
at $1.95 each .... $..........

.... **HOW TO CATCH STEELHEAD**
at $1.95 each .... $..........

.... **HOW TO CATCH TROUT**
at $1.95 each .... $..........

.... **HOW TO HUNT DEER AND OTHER GAME**
at $1.95 each .... $..........

.... **LOGGING ROAD TRAVEL**
Vol. 1 -- VICTORIA TO CAMPBELL RIVER
at $3.95 each .... $..........

.... **LOGGING ROAD TRAVEL**
Vol. 2 -- CAMPBELL RIVER TO CAPE SCOTT
at $2.95 each .... $..........

.... **OUTDOORS WITH ALEC MERRIMAN**
at $2.95 each .... $..........

.... **OKANAGAN BACKROADS**
Vol. 1 -- SOUTH - CENTRAL OKANAGAN
at $3.95 each .... $..........

.... **OKANAGAN BACK ROADS**
Vol. 2 -- NORTH OKANAGAN - SHUSWAP
at $3.95 each .... $..........

.... **TAKE A TRIP -- ACCORDING TO DOYLE**
at $1.50 each .... $..........

Continued next page

.... **HOW TO ESCAPE THE RAT RACE**
at $1.25 each .... $..........

.... **HOW TO CHOOSE YOUR BOOZE**
at $1.50 each .... $..........

.... **HOW TO WIN AT THE STOCK MARKET**
at $2.00 each .... $..........

.... **BUCKTAILS AND HOOCHIES**
at $1.95 each .... $ ....

.... **50 CASSEROLES FOR DRUNKS**
at .95 each .... $ ....

.... **PRINCE GEORGE BACKROADS**
at $3.95 each .... $..........

.... **CRUISE SHIPS — INSIDE STORY**
at $3.95 each .... $..........

.... **MICROWAVE COOKING**
at $2.95 each .... $..........

.... **CRUISING THE INLAND SEA**
at $3.95 each .... $ ....

TOTAL ENCLOSED $..........

**SALTAIRE PUBLISHING LTD., P.O. BOX 2003
SIDNEY, B.C., CANADA V8L 3S3**

SEND TO:

NAME ....

ADDRESS ....APT. NO. ....

CITY ....PROVINCE/STATE ....

POSTAL CODE/ZIP CODE ....

NOTES

NOTES

NOTES

NOTES

NOTES

NOTES

NOTES

NOTES

Horne Lake road – go
advice @ Info centre
Parksville.